LIVING LANTERNS

ALSO WRITTEN AND ILLUSTRATED
BY HILDA SIMON

Partners, Guests, and Parasites
Feathers, Plain and Fancy
Insect Masquerades

LIVING

Written and illustrated

LANTERNS

Luminescence in Animals

by Hilda Simon

THE VIKING PRESS   NEW YORK

ACKNOWLEDGMENTS

I gratefully acknowledge the aid I have received from various persons and sources in the preparation of this book. I especially wish to thank Dr. J. Grober of Bad Bodendorf, Germany, for supplying pertinent material; my friends at the Zeiss Optical Works in Germany for some rare photographs of luminescent animals; Miss Nina J. Root, librarian at the Museum of Natural History, for her help in finding the research material I needed; and Dr. René Catala, whose book *Carnival Under the Sea* gave me most of my information on fluorescent deep-sea corals.

My very special thanks go to Mrs. Beatrice Rosenfeld, science editor of The Viking Press, whose invaluable help with the manuscript I greatly appreciate, and whose untiring efforts made it a pleasure to work on this book.

Contents

Light in the Night

One of the momentous advances in early man's development was his successful conversion of fire from a fearful and destructive force to a highly useful servant of his everyday needs. From that time on, primitive men were able to warm themselves in cold weather, cook their food, shape and harden their weapons and tools, and, finally, illuminate the darkness. Man thus progressed to a level of independence from his environment not available to animals, which are forced to adjust their lives to the climate and to the light provided by the sun, the moon, and the stars.

Because of the importance of having "light in the night," the role of fire for illumination had to be separated from the uses of its heat. The search for better, more efficient ways of illuminating the darkness began in ancient times and continued through the centuries.

Many early civilizations used long-burning torches which could be placed in holders. Then came simple whale-oil lamps and candles, made of tallow or wax and fitted with slow-burning wicks. Candles remained the chief source of artificial light for many centuries. Only in the nineteenth century did candles give way to such innovations as the petroleum lamp, illuminating gas, and, late in the century, the great advance in artificial light: the incandescent bulb.

All the earlier sources of light were extremely dangerous. The chance of fires is always great with open flames, flammable liquids, and combustible gases. Electric light had a number of advantages: it was clean, relatively safe, and much more efficient; instead of using flammable material, light was produced by an electric current heating a filament to an incandescent glow.

Despite this big step forward, scientists continued to search for more efficient light sources. A few decades ago, the fluorescent lamp was designed for commercial use. It soon replaced the incandescent light in offices and plants as a cheaper source of light. The fluorescent tube contains mercury vapor that gives off ultraviolet light when excited by an electric discharge. Coating the inside of the tube is a phosphor powder that glows in the presence of ultraviolet radiation.

Even though fluorescent lamps produce light less expensively than incandescent lamps, the light is by no means really efficient. Some energy is wasted in heat to produce the electric discharge in the tube. It has been the dream of engineers working in this field to find a method of producing truly efficient, *cold* light for commercial use. So far, none of the attempts has been economically feasible.

This is especially tantalizing in view of the fact that cold light found in nature has been the subject of intensive research for the past fifty years. Both inorganic and organic cold-light sources have been closely studied, for cold light is produced by certain chemicals as well as by many living organisms, both plant and animal.

Because light was always so important to man, it is not surprising that "living light" was a source of wonder and fascination to people even in ancient times. Geographic location had much to do with observations involving light-emitting organisms, which can be divided roughly into two large groups: those found in the ocean, and those on the land, usually in areas that are moist or heavily wooded. Hence peoples living in comparatively arid regions had little chance of seeing light-producing animals.

The earliest written records of such observations are about 2500 years old and come from China. In the West, the Greek philosopher Aristotle was the first to mention various kinds of light-giving organisms. Strangely enough, very little about this phenomenon is found in Roman literature, and only a few references to animals that shine in the night can be found in the literature of the Middle Ages. In the fifteenth and sixteenth centuries, however, the great age of modern exploration began. With it came observations—often in great detail—made by the explorers during their voyages. Thus Columbus tells of a strange light in the ocean which he noticed just shortly before landing on what he thought to be India, and Sir Francis Drake, the famed English navigator and admiral, wrote about the large tropical fire beetles he saw in the New World.

Quite naturally, in all the early reports fact was mixed with some fiction, and the various types of cold light were not distinguished from one another—the phosphorescence of minerals, the glow of rotting wood, the eerie light given off by dead sea animals, and the light emitted by living creatures such as jellyfish and fireflies. Aristotle, for example, explained some of the strange light in the night as the tendency of "smooth things" to shine in the dark. Naturalists of those times believed in the false notion that some birds gave off light. Also universal was the belief that the eyes of many animals could produce light. Because the nature of light in general was not understood, no one realized that eyes that seem to shine in the night are merely reflecting light.

The first book devoted entirely to light emitted without production of heat was written by Konrad von Gesner, a sixteenth-century German naturalist, and signaled the beginning of serious scientific inquiry into this phenomenon. In England Sir Francis Bacon was very much interested in such light. Noting the colors produced by burning substances, he observed that such flames were never green, but that the "light most inclined to greenishness is that of the firefly."

In the following century, the noted English physicist Robert Boyle became greatly interested in the luminescence of various substances and made experiments with shining wood. Much was learned about the nature of light through the work of Boyle's great contemporaries, Sir Isaac Newton in England and Christiaan Huygens in Holland. The search for the many still-unanswered mysteries of this phenomenon gained impetus in the subsequent centuries and was encouraged by a number of European institutes of higher learning.

By the end of the nineteenth century, a great deal had been learned about the nature of "living light." Scientists were now able to distinguish between light produced by fungi or bacteria and that emitted by animals, such as deep-sea fish and fireflies. They also had discovered that living organisms required oxygen to produce light. And in 1888, the term "luminescence" was coined by a German physicist, Eilhardt Wiedemann, to describe "all those phenomena of light which are not solely conditioned by a rise in temperature." Wiedemann thus contrasted luminescence to incandescence, or "hot light," in which solids or liquids heated to increasingly higher temperatures emit shorter wave lengths that become visible to the eyes, first as "red-hot" and then as "white-hot" light.

Luminescence includes phosphorescence and fluorescence of inorganic substances which glow when exposed to such radiation as an electron beam or ultraviolet rays, and bioluminescence, the ability of living organisms to emit light. It is the latter, and especially bioluminescence of animals, rather than that of plants, which this book is going to explore.

The plants capable of producing light are all of a type known as fungi, which are characterized by their lack of chlorophyll, the coloring matter of all green plants. As we know, green plants give off oxygen during the process of photosynthesis, absorbing energy from sunlight to produce carbohydrates from carbon dioxide and water. Fungi, on the other hand, need different conditions to live and never give off oxygen.

Mushrooms that glow in the dark with an eerie light are found in many parts of the world and have been known for a long time. What was not known until the twentieth century is that the glow of rotting wood —a phenomenon noted by Aristotle more than 2000 years ago—is also caused by luminescent fungus growths which live on the decaying wood.

Many other familiar instances of "light in the night" are caused by luminescent bacteria. These tiny light-giving organisms are responsible for the strange light that can be seen on dead fish and other dead or dying marine creatures that have been washed ashore, for most luminescent bacteria are found in the ocean, apparently needing salt water to thrive. Living animals infested by luminous bacteria frequently have been thought to be self-luminescent, until the cause of the luminescence was established. Infestation with luminous bacteria is a disease which eventually kills the host animal, except in those cases where a symbiotic relationship exists between such bacteria and their host.

Within the past decades, research on bioluminescence has been accelerated and has yielded an enormous amount of information about how cold light is produced by many creatures, although not all types of luminescent animals have been studied and many details of the basic process still remain to be resolved.

What scientists have found out about the way bioluminescence is produced is fully as fascinating as the phenomenon itself. But before exploring the scientific solution of this age-old mystery, let us first take a look at the many wondrous creatures on land and in the ocean that are capable of producing cold light, using their built-in lamps for a variety of purposes.

Flying Flashlights

The warm and velvety darkness of a midsummer night, when the air is calm and filled with the scent of night-blooming blossoms, is a very special kind of darkness. All it needs to round out the *Midsummer Night's Dream* quality are the bright pin-point flashes of fireflies gleaming in grass and bushes and against the midnight blue of the sky.

A large number of popular names for a particular animal is a sure indication that it has been of interest not only to naturalists, but also to the ordinary inhabitants of a region. Common insects that are either injurious or beneficial, or that have unusual habits or characteristics, almost always have local nicknames in the various countries where they occur. The praying mantis and the lady beetle are good examples. Fireflies are no exception. They are known as glowworms, as lightning bugs, and, in parts of Europe, as St.-John's-worms. The last-named term derives from the coincidence that St. John the Baptist's Day is celebrated on June 24, a time when certain species of fireflies have completed their metamorphoses and begin their brief lives as adult insects by seeking mates. Old Nordic and Germanic legends merged with Christian beliefs to make St. John's Eve the night when fires were lit on mountainsides. Originally, in pre-Christian times, these fires were lit in Europe to celebrate the summer solstice, when the days are the longest in the year. Later, the "St. John's fires," as the rites were then called, were believed to ward off bad luck, evil spells, and illness. By the same token, the St.-John's-worms with their tiny bright lights were considered harbingers of good luck and health, and years of bad luck would be in store for anyone who killed them. The population of those regions would not have taken kindly to scientific experiments in which millions of fireflies were deliberately killed in order to find out how their light is produced.

The literature on fireflies far exceeds that on any other group of luminous animals. In the regions where fireflies are common, the phenomenon of these tiny "living lamps" has intrigued man for many centuries. Both the poet and the scientist, each in his own way, have studied, observed, and written about these small insects.

Twenty-five hundred years ago, the ancient Chinese

believed that decaying grass and other vegetation miraculously turned into fireflies. Strange as this notion seems to us, it does prove that the Chinese noted accurately that fireflies prefer moist, damp habitats. In the fourth century B.C., Aristotle, the great Greek philosopher and naturalist, gave a good description of fireflies. So did the Roman author and naturalist Pliny the Elder, who lived in the first century A.D.

In 1638 Carolus Vintimillia, an Italian naturalist who lived in Palermo, noted that male fireflies had wings, while females, although wingless, had been compensated for that lack by a "more vigorous light in order that they could call the males at night with their shine."

Vintimillia's observations were only partially correct. This is not surprising, for the problem of distinguishing the sex in various species of fireflies with winged or wingless females is confusing today, even for the experts.

What exactly are fireflies? Despite their popular name, they are neither flies nor bugs—and certainly not worms—but true beetles. They belong to the large order of Coleoptera, literally "sheath-winged." The scientific name refers to the fact that these insects, in contrast to such members of the insect class as bees, flies, and butterflies, have a hard or leathery pair of anterior wings that has developed into a protective cover for the posterior, membranous pair.

Fireflies are members of the family Lampyridae, which in turn is a part of the suborder of Malacodermatidae, or soft-skinned beetles. And indeed, their "soft

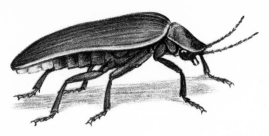

Male of Photinus pyralis, *a common North American firefly.*

skin"—the lack of the hard exoskeleton that distinguishes most other beetles—is an outstanding characteristic of these insects.

Rarely exceeding half an inch in length, fireflies are elongated and flattened, with a prothorax that extends, shieldlike, in a semicircle over a downturned head. Their eyes are large and their antennae thin, a sure indication that these insects rely on sight rather than on sound vibrations in finding their goal. In contrast, many other insects, such as some moths and certain members of the scarab-beetle family, have large, often feathery or comblike antennae, which serve as sensitive sound-receiving stations that help them find their mates.

Leathery wing covers protect the firefly's soft abdomen, which bears the light organs on its underside. Arrangement, size, and number of these organs, which appear yellowish in daylight, vary considerably among the different species, and even between the sexes of the same species. Generally, however, they are arranged either in pairs along the sides of the abdomen, or as a single large organ extending over several segments.

Fireflies usually have rather dull, drab colors. Most of them appear brownish or grayish in daylight, often with reddish areas on the prothorax. Even most tropical kinds are not brightly colored; their special lighting equipment makes them creatures of the darkness, relatively inactive and undistinguished during the daytime.

Fireflies are found in almost every part of the world except arid and polar regions. Although there are many genera and hundreds of different species, each with its own characteristics, all of them are very similar in appearance. The differences among the various species are found mainly in such features as size and number of

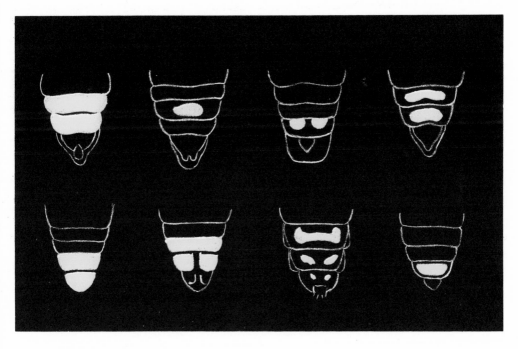

Number and arrangement of light organs differ considerably among the various species of fireflies.

light organs, winged or wingless females, dark or luminous larvae, and the eating habits of the adults.

As larvae, all fireflies are carnivorous, feeding mainly on snails and slugs. This explains these insects' preference for the moist habitats where such mollusks can be found. A few larvae even live in the water, evidently having developed the ability to store enough oxygen in their bodies to permit prolonged underwater activity.

Firefly larvae have pointed, pincer-like mandibles with which they can attack even large snails. When the larva bites its victim, it pierces the skin and injects a small amount of a powerful digestive fluid. The accumulated fluid from repeated bites seems to have a paralyzing effect on the snail. At any rate, observations have shown that most of the attacked mollusks become

A firefly larva attacking a snail. Its shell offers the snail no protection against this enemy.

quite motionless. Soon the injected parts of the snail turn into a sticky, brownish mass upon which the larva can feed.

Some firefly species seem to prefer particular kinds of snails. Because one local species of firefly preys on a snail which harbors organisms dangerous to man, Japanese scientists some years ago launched a campaign to protect the firefly. The effort was not successful, however, since in Japan, as in most other civilized countries today, the excessive use of pesticides has sharply reduced the number of all kinds of flying insects. In addition, immoderate collecting of fireflies for scientific experiments has taken a tremendous toll among the "lightning bugs."

Relatively little is known about the diet of adult fireflies. Observations by different naturalists have revealed what appear to be widely varying eating habits. The adults of some species do not seem to take any food at all; others are evidently as carnivorous as their larvae, preying on various insects that in some cases include the adults of other firefly species.

Very confusing in the identification of a particular species is the fact that the female's ability to fly and the male's ability to produce light vary with the species. In some species the adult males and females are both winged *and* luminous. Mostly, as Vintimillia observed three hundred years ago, the females are wingless. They are the "glowworms" of poetry. Such grublike, flightless females almost always have the stronger light. In a few species, the males have no light organs at all,

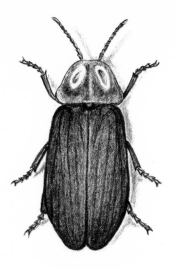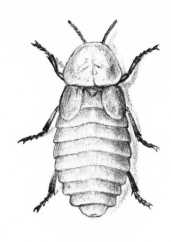

Male and wingless female of Lampyris splendidula, *the common small firefly of central Europe.*

but this never seems to be true of the females. The males of those species in which both sexes are winged have larger light organs than the females, which is a reversal of the general rule.

The glowworm of song and story belongs to the genus *Lampyris*. Two species, *Lampyris noctiluca* and *Lampyris splendidula*, whose females are wingless, occur in northern and central Europe. They are similar except for the larger size of *noctiluca* and a difference in the number of females' light organs. The female of *noctiluca* has two large and four small light organs, while that of *splendidula* has one large and thirteen small ones. Males of both species have only two, which are somewhat larger in the *noctiluca* species.

In Italy and other parts of southern Europe, the local fireflies belong to the genus *Luciola*. It is interesting to note that, halfway around the world, the Japanese species belong to this same genus. North American and Caribbean fireflies, on the other hand, are all members of the genera *Photuris* and *Photinus*.

Among all species whose adults of both sexes are luminous, a fairly complicated system of signaling exists. This clearly distinguishes the male firefly's flash from the female's answer and is necessary in order to avoid one male's being attracted by the signal of another male. Insofar as we can tell from observations, this is accomplished by the timing of the flashes as well as by the shape, and possibly the brilliance, of the luminous area.

Lampyris noctiluca, *the large firefly of central Europe. The larviform female is the glowworm of song and story.*

Observations of *Photinus pyralis*, a common North American species, have shown that there is an interval of two seconds between the flash of the male and the answering flash of the female. This holds true only, however, for a temperature of approximately 76 degrees Fahrenheit. A rise in temperature causes a quickening of the pace at which the flashes take place, while cooler temperatures slow it down. Thus eight flashes and answers per minute at a temperature of 68 degrees have been reported as compared to exactly twice that number at a temperature of 80 degrees. Warmth also increases the brilliance and changes the color of the emitted light, which turns more yellowish as the temperature rises. At 110 degrees, however, the light assumes a reddish tinge and then is extinguished altogether.

In certain regions where fireflies abound, large groups of them may synchronize their flashes, providing a truly magnificent spectacle of natural pyrotechnics. In Asia, for example, one naturalist reported that all the fireflies on a particular tree flashed in unison up to a hundred times a minute, lighting up the tree at intervals of only a little more than half a second—like some kind of magic Christmas tree. Simultaneously, another tree some distance away with its own resident firefly population also lit up a hundred times per minute, its living flashlights fully synchronized among themselves but not with those of the other trees in the neighborhood. Small wonder that observers fortunate enough to have seen such a spectacle can hardly find words that adequately express its beauty.

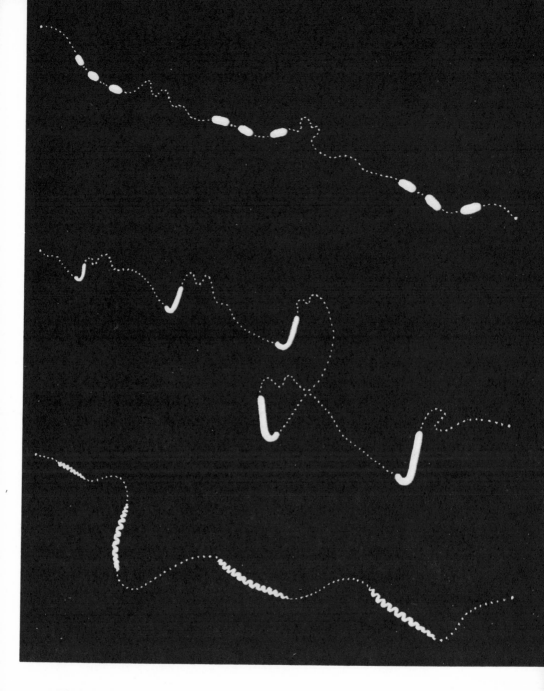

Flash patterns of the males of three species of fireflies belonging to the genus Photinus, *as studied and recorded by Dr. James E. Lloyd of the University of Florida.*

Male and fully winged female of Photinus pallens, *a common Jamaican firefly.*

Even in areas where fireflies do not synchronize their flashes but occur in great numbers, the effect of thousands of bright, twinkling stars studding the darkness of a summer night turns sober naturalists into poets. Thus Paul A. Zahl, of the *National Geographic Magazine,* describes a performance in the rugged heights of the Blue Mountains of Jamaica, which is known among entomologists for its abundance of luminous insects. More than fifty firefly species have been found on the island. Dr. Zahl noted that once the display had got under way, it gradually built up until it became "a brilliance that filled the air and spangled the foliage."

The most common Jamaican species observed by Dr.

Zahl has winged females. However, they do not fly around very much, especially at night; they are satisfied to sit in bushes and wait for the males to find them. Although bigger than the male, the female of this species has smaller eyes, shorter wings, and only one lighted abdominal segment, whereas the male has two.

Adult fireflies have a short life span. After having spent up to two years as larvae, the mature beetles have only a few days or, at most, weeks to fulfill the important function of propagating their kind. After mating, the females deposit their eggs in moist crannies and then die.

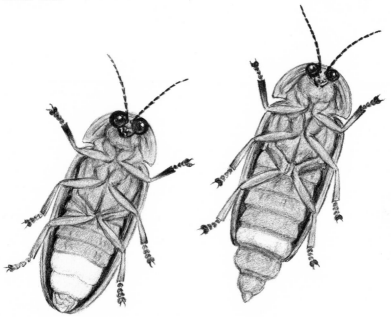

The undersides of both sexes of Photinus pallens *with light organs. Those of the smaller male cover two abdominal segments, those of the female only one.*

The color of the fireflies' light differs slightly with the species but is usually greenish-white or yellowish, with wave lengths varying between 540 and 620 millimicrons (a millimicron is a millionth of a millimeter and a standard unit for measuring light). Our visible spectrum ranges from approximately 700 millimicrons for the long wave lengths of red light to 380 millimicrons for the short violet waves. Most firefly light thus has the median wave length usually attributed to white light, which is set at 550 millimicrons.

Fireflies are the most common, the most abundant, and the most universally distributed of all the "flying flashlights." There are, however, a number of other insects that carry their own lanterns while flying through the night. The most spectacular and the most famous of these are the beetles of the genus *Pyrophorus*, which belong to the family of Elateridae, commonly known as click beetles. These beetles are distinguished by the way in which they are able to right themselves when they land on their backs. After lying quietly for a little while, a click beetle suddenly flips itself into the air by means of a prong on its thorax which fits into a groove on the first segment of its abdomen. As the prong slides home, there is a loud clicking noise, which has given the family its popular name. Frequently the beetle lands on its feet with the first try; otherwise, it tries again.

Ordinary click beetles are found in almost every part of the world, but the luminous members of the group, known as fire beetles, are confined mainly to the Amer-

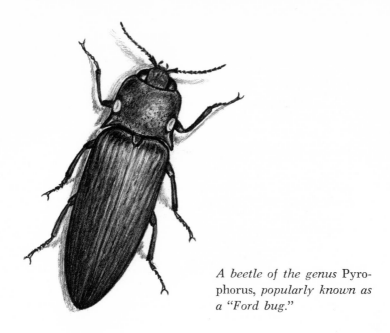

A beetle of the genus Pyrophorus, *popularly known as a "Ford bug."*

icas and especially to South and Central America. These beetles are much larger than fireflies, averaging nearly one inch in length, although some are smaller and a few, the giants of the clan, attain a length of two inches or more. Of the dozens of species known to naturalists, many are not brightly luminous, but some emit light of a brilliance unmatched by other luminous beetles. The main source of luminescence in the *Pyrophorus* beetles is not found on the abdomen, as in fireflies, but in two roundish yellow spots, one on each side of the prothorax. These spots glow in the dark with a bright light which may vary in hue from whitish to a greenish-yellow, depending on the species and also on the age of the individual beetle. Several species have an additional luminous area at the base of the abdomen which emits

Pyrophorus does not flash its lights as fireflies do; instead, its two thoracic "headlights" glow steadily.

an orange or even reddish light. These beetles are often popularly called automobile bugs or Ford bugs, names which are especially appropriate for a species that sports two large "headlights" and a smaller red "taillight."

The light emitted by the larger fire beetles is so bright that only one or two of them make it possible to read a wrist watch on a dark night. Half a dozen individuals of one of the larger species provide enough light to read a book. Once, when all other light sources in a Central American hospital had failed, a number of these beetles placed in a glass jar were used to supply light for a successful emergency operation.

Many native women in Central and South America use the fire beetles as striking ornaments when they go to a dance at night. Caught alive and placed in small gauze bags, the insects are fastened in the hair along with other adornments, providing a most unusual and attractive type of jewelry.

A very practical use for the light of fire beetles has been found by the Indians inhabiting certain jungle regions of South America. Transparent bags are filled with these insects and tied around the ankles of the natives when they go out at night. Thus their paths are illuminated and they can make their way through dense undergrowth in a jungle which, because of its almost-solid canopy of treetops, is dark even on moonlit nights.

Other luminous beetles belong to the genus *Phengodes* and related genera. *Phengodes laticollis,* a South American species, is interesting in that the winged male gives off little light, while both the larva and the larviform, wingless female are capable of spectacular "firework" displays. In the following chapter we will discuss both these and the larva of another beetle with the tongue-twisting name of *Phrixothrix.* The adult winged male *Phrixothrix* is luminous, emitting a diffuse glow from light organs located on both sides of the abdomen. The light is most pronounced if the beetle is handled or otherwise stimulated.

The story of flying luminous insects would not be complete without inclusion of a few controversial cases, the best known of which are the lantern and candle flies. Again, these insects are not flies: they are true bugs. Found in South America and Asia, respectively, they are relatives of the cicadas. *Fulgora lanternaria,* the lantern fly, is also often called the alligator bug, from the grotesque enlargement of its proboscis, or snout, which is almost as long as the rest of its body and is marked with dark lines and blotches which suggest the head of an alligator, complete with eyes, nostrils, and teeth.

Controversy has swirled around this peculiar creature for centuries. Older naturalists reported it to luminesce from the large snout. Later this was categorically denied by other naturalists, among them the famed English entomologist Henry Bates. Today, about two thirds of the entomologists still doubt the insect's ability to give off light, while one third are convinced it does.

The difficulty is that no one has ever been able to prove light emission by this bug. Nobody has ever photographed a lantern fly with a shining lantern, and despite careful examination of the tissues of the snout, it has not been possible to find evidence of any typical light organ. In fact, the snout is hollow and in no way resembles the light-producing tissues of other luminescent insects.

The first report of its alleged luminescence came from a remarkable woman, Maria Sybille Merian, who was both an artist and a nature lover. She lived from 1647 to 1717 and was the daughter of an engraver. Born in Frankfurt-on-the-Main, Germany, she showed an early talent for drawing insects and flowers and became quite famous as an artist. At the age of fifty-

The odd-looking alligator bug has often been reported to be lumines-cent, but so far this has not been proven.

two, accompanied by one of her two daughters, she undertook the long, uncomfortable, and risky journey to Dutch Guiana, or Surinam, as it was then called. There she and her daughter created a number of beautifully colored and detailed paintings of local flowers, butterflies, and cicadas. After her return to Germany she published a book of these paintings and an accompanying text in Latin under the title *Meta-morphosis Insectorum Surinamensis*. In her book she mentions that during her stay in South America, the natives whom she had hired to collect various caterpillars and other small creatures for her once brought her a number of the unusual-looking lantern flies. She reports that she placed these insects in a box and was awakened at night by loud scrambling noises. When she opened the box, "flames came out," as she put it. The insects, she wrote, had "all lighted as if they were on fire."

It has been suggested that the reason no proof of the lantern flies' luminescence has so far been secured is the limited period in which the light may be seen. Naturalists who believe in the luminescence of these insects think they emit light only at certain times—probably only during the mating period—and then not unless males and females are together. It will be interesting to watch for conclusive proof either for or against these theories, thus resolving a centuries-old nature mystery. The same holds true for the Chinese candle fly, which has a very long, thin, beaklike snout, and about which reports of alleged luminescence also persist.

A number of flying insects from a variety of families have at one time or another been credited with the ability to produce light. Most of these reports have proved false, or at least deceptive. There are, for example, certain gnats which have been found to shine with an eerie light. Close examination, however, showed these insects to be infected with luminous bacteria, which after a while killed their hosts. So far, flying insects whose luminescence in the adult is proved without a doubt are restricted to the order Coleoptera.

With a single exception, there have been no reliable reports of luminescence among members of the huge order of Lepidoptera, the moths and butterflies. Several naturalists, observing the habits of the great tiger moth, described how this insect, when handled and thus irritated, secreted a luminous substance. Other naturalists claim, however, that this secretion, which is very oily and colored a bright golden yellow, may have reflected light from another source. The question of the luminosity in this instance has not yet been settled.

It is a different story with the larval stages of flying insects. In the next chapter we will examine in detail a number of most unusual luminous insect larvae as well as other light-producing land creatures.

Lights That Creep and Crawl

Fireflies and fire beetles are by far the best known, the most often observed and closely studied, and the most definitely "certified" of all luminescent land animals. By that we mean that no question at all exists about their self-luminescence, that their light organs have been examined and extensive tests made to determine the anatomy of this luminescence.

Many flightless light-emitting creatures are simply larval forms of fireflies and other flying insects, or else mature but wingless females that can hardly be distinguished from the grubs. There are, nevertheless, a considerable number of other insects and insect relatives that have been found to be genuinely self-luminous. The term "self-luminous" indicates the existence of

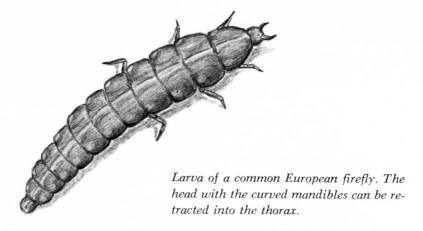

Larva of a common European firefly. The head with the curved mandibles can be retracted into the thorax.

light-producing organs or tissues, in contrast to luminosity stemming from an infection by luminous bacteria.

Among firefly larvae, the ability to produce light differs with the species. Some have no light organs to begin with and develop them only during the pupal stage; others, upon hatching, emit light every bit as

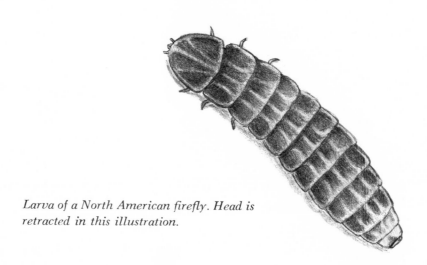

Larva of a North American firefly. Head is retracted in this illustration.

bright as that of the adults. Most of them are luminous to some degree, and a few seem to be luminescent even before hatching, although this light cannot normally be seen because of lightproof egg shells.

Why these larvae should be luminous is something of a mystery if we accept the theory that the light of

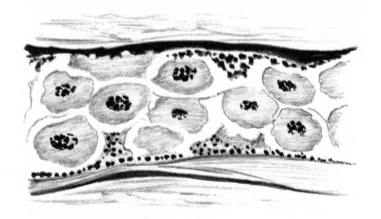

Light organ of a fire beetle larva.

fireflies is the instrument by which the sexes attract and find each other in the darkness, as the larvae are sexless and have no reason for attracting one another. Some observers have offered the suggestion that the light of the grubs may serve as a sort of warning signal to potential enemies and thus provide a deterrent to attack by certain predators. This theory, which is analagous to the concept of "warning coloration" (bright color patterns displayed by unpalatable butterflies and other insects as protection against enemies), has been somewhat weakened by actual observations. Both frogs

Glowing with a greenish-yellow light after a meal of fireflies, this grass frog seems unaffected by its temporary luminosity.

and toads, which are the fireflies' main enemies because they share the same damp habitats, do not seem to have been deterred at all by the strange light emanating from the grubs—or from the adults, for that matter. On the contrary, in several instances frogs and toads were found to have stuffed themselves with fireflies and their larvae. The results of these glowing meals were glowing amphibians: the light emitted by the large number of victims the frog or toad had swallowed shone brightly and steadily, as firefly light will when the insect is in great distress, through the partly transparent tissues of the predator's belly until the fireflies were completely digested.

Among all earth-bound light-givers, none are more fascinating than the larvae of some of the beetles mentioned in the preceding chapter. The grubs of both *Phrixothrix* and *Phengodes*, as well as those of some related beetles, are unusal among all luminous land creatures in that they emit light of different colors from the anterior and posterior parts of their bodies. From the head of *Phrixothrix* comes a bright red glow, and eleven pairs of light organs along the sides produce a greenish-yellow light. The combination of the red "headlight" and the rows of small side lights makes these larvae look like miniature trains as they move slowly through the darkness, explaining the popular English and Spanish names, railroad worm and *ferrocarril*, respectively.

The favorite position of the railroad worm is curled up so that the head almost touches the tail end. Photographs taken by its own light show the unusually bright glow emitted by this sluggish, grub-like creature. In daylight it looks singularly undistinguished and unattractive and bears a striking resemblance to the "wireworms" that so often plague farmers by destroying sprouting wheat and other grain plants. By night, however, *Phrixothrix* turns into an insect Cinderella as it is transformed from a drab brown worm

By daylight the Phrixothrix *looks like most other beetle grubs.*

into a display of glowing colored lights.

The female of *Phrixothrix* is practically indistinguishable from the larva and was in fact often mistaken for the latter until naturalists observed some of these larviform females mating with adult males. At no point does the winged male ever attain the brightness of the land-bound larval and female *Phrixothrix* specimens.

The red headlight of this insect has aroused considerable interest among naturalists because it is a relatively rare color for light produced by luminescent land organisms. Only *Phrixothrix, Phengodes,* and related

The Phrixothrix *larve at night becomes the "railroad worm," with its red "headlight" and rows of brilliant yellow lights.*

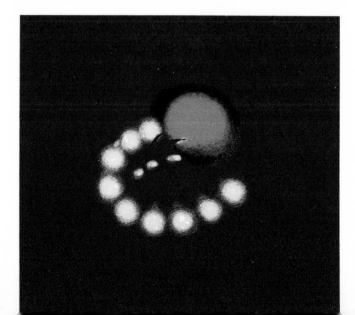

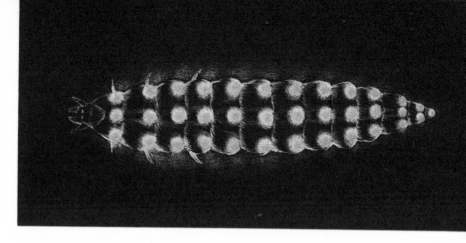

The star worm of Singapore glows at night with three rows of bright lights.

species display red light in addition to the common greenish-yellow light emitted by the majority of these creatures. It was thought at one time that the tissues of the head of these larvae contained a red transparent pigment which acted as a filter for the light emitted by the anterior light organ, and which transmitted only the red wave lengths, absorbing the rest. However, this speculation proved wrong: there is no red pigment at all in the tissues of the head, although red pigment has been found in the abdomen of the grub. This means that these larvae are actually capable of emitting light of differing wave lengths from different parts of the body at the same time.

In the Far East, the larva of a nonluminous beetle presents a display of luminescence that, although all the emitted light is of the same color, is described to be so beautiful that, once seen, it is never forgotten. The insect is known as the star worm, or diamond worm, and has been found in the area around Singapore. Two inches in length, the star worm has not just two, but three rows of light organs running the entire length of the body, one row on each side and the third along the center. The light is a bright greenish-blue. The adults are drab beetles without any unusual or attractive features.

Very interesting to students of bioluminescence are the larvae of certain small flies, especially those of a group known as fungus gnats. These insects are similar to midges, which in turn are frequently confused with mosquitoes, which they resemble. Fungus gnats get their name from their larvae's habit of living among fungi and decaying vegetation. Some of them become a nuisance in cellars where mushrooms are grown for human consumption, as the gnats spin webs among the edible fungi to trap the tiny insects upon which they feed, thus ruining the mushroom crop.

Larvae of fungus gnats are usually white with dark, chitinized heads. The larva of a North American species, *Playtura fultoni*, found in the Appalachian Mountains of North Carolina, spins its web in moist, dark crevices. At night the grub is luminous, emitting a bluish light from the anterior portion of its body. It also sports a tiny "taillight." The adult gnat has no luminescence at all.

Playtura does not turn its light off and on in the manner of fireflies. Instead it lets its light shine steadily all through the night, but never during daytime. It keeps to this rhythm even if conditions are altered artificially by keeping the insect in darkness for several days. It is believed that the light helps attract the small insects that are *Playtura*'s natural prey. In this case, the light undoubtedly is very helpful in the larva's quest for food. We should not, however, assume on the strength of this one example that this is the rule among luminous gnat larvae. A European species, *Ceroplatus*, also has luminescent larvae even though the latter feed exclusively on decaying vegetation. *Ceroplatus* is found in Sweden, where the larva spins its web on the underside of mushrooms. No explanation for the luminescence of these larvae has been advanced; the adults, as in all other species of gnats, are completely nonluminous at all times.

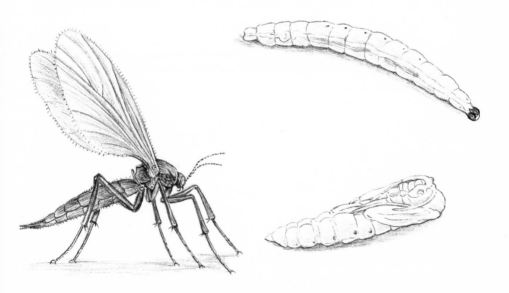

A tiny fungus gnat in different stages of development. The larvae of several species are capable of emitting light, but the adults are all nonluminous.

Probably the most famous of all the light-producing fly larvae is found in New Zealand. Several related species are native to nearby Tasmania. The earliest reports of the "New Zealand glowworm," as the larva is commonly called, were given in 1886 by two explorers, one a Maori chieftain and the other an Englishman, who found these insects in a huge cave called Waitomo, a Maori word meaning "water entering a hole." What these men described is a mass display of luminescence so overwhelming that, according to many visitors who have since been inside Waitomo, it must be seen to be appreciated. The darkness of the cave, through which runs a rather muddy underground river, is illuminated by the glow emanating from countless small fly larvae which hang suspended on sticky threads from the walls and the vaulted roof. Each larva, which is less than an inch long, emits a rather faint bluish light. By itself, the individual insect would not in any way be a remarkable example of luminescence. Waitomo, however, is a mass display, and all the lights are "turned on" at the same time. With hundreds of thousands or even millions of these tiny suspended lights glowing in the cave, the effect is spectacular, and it is admired each year by many tourists who are taken into the cave by boat. The tourists are advised to remain quiet during that underground journey. The fly larvae, it seems, are extremely sensitive to sound and react promptly to unusual noises by turning off their lights as suddenly as though a switch had been thrown. Evidently the grubs equate unknown sounds with danger and prefer

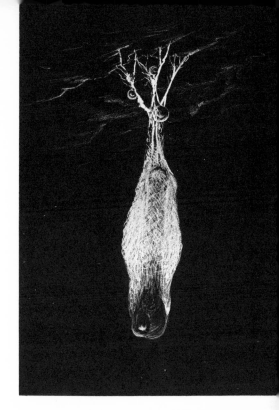

Close-up of Arachnocampa luminosa *grub shows cocoon suspended by the sticky threads which trap the prey attracted by the grub's light.*

to remain dark until they feel safe once again.

The adult of the New Zealand glowworm has no popular name. Its scientific species name, *Arachnocampa luminosa,* refers to the luminescence of the larval stage. During the pupal stage, their light, which earlier shone so steadily, becomes intermittent. When the adult insect emerges, it no longer has any luminescence if it is a male fly. The sex of the flies can, in fact, be told several days before emergence, because the cocoons containing males turn dark at a time when those containing females are still luminescent. The latter stay faintly luminous for about two days after leaving the pupal cocoon, and then they also lose any ability to produce light. However, from the eggs they lay, luminous grubs will hatch and spin their threads and continue to provide the magic illumination for "Glowworm Grotto," to the delight of visitors from many countries.

The light emitted by the *Arachnocampa* larvae undoubtedly serves as a lure, attracting the small insects on which the predaceous fly grubs feed. Once the prey touches the sticky threads from which the treacherous attractive lights are suspended, it is a ready victim for the waiting grub. These fly larvae thus catch their prey in the accepted manner of spiders capturing flies, adding only the sophisticated touch of a shining lure.

Flightless luminescent creatures are by no means limited to the larval forms of flying insects. There are a number of self-luminous land-bound species that possess the ability to give off light. Prominent among nonflying insects are primitive members of the insect class known as springtails. These peculiar, usually minute creatures occur in most regions of the world—even in the polar areas, where they are called "snow fleas."

Very little is known about the life histories of springtails. We do know that they are often found under damp leaves and generally in moist localities. They feed on vegetation and occasionally damage cultivated plants.

Springtails average less than one-eighth of an inch in length. They are aptly named, for they possess a spring-like mechanism on the underside of their abdomens which permits them to be agile jumpers. Although this causes them to resemble fleas, they are in no way

These tiny springtails are among the most primitive of all insects.

related to these bloodsuckers.

A number of luminous springtail species are known, most of which occur in Europe, especially in Germany. Near Heidelberg, a species only one-sixteenth of an inch long was observed in piles of moist leaves and humus. Disturbing such a pile in the dark made the dead leaves come alive with scores of tiny, twinkling, jumping lights.

The self-luminescence of springtails has been established beyond any doubt. This is not true of luminous ants and wasps, reports of which turn up from time to time, but which are believed to be cases of infection with luminous bacteria. We have to look outside the insect group of crawlers to find other undisputed instances of genuine luminosity. Foremost among these are the centipedes, which belong to a large group known to biologists as Chilopoda. These many-legged creatures, which usually have a lot fewer than the hundred legs suggested by their name, are often mistakenly referred to as insects. Anyone who knows the basic facts about insects will remember that they have only six legs, even though some larval forms, such as caterpillars, may have additional false legs called prolegs.

The largest, most colorful and bizarre-looking centipedes occur in the tropics, where the most poisonous of these peculiar creatures also are found. One outstanding feature of centipedes is the modification of the anterior pair of legs into poison fangs. In some of the large tropical kinds, the bite is extremely painful and occasionally fatal even to man. The venom of certain species is held to be more potent than that of most poisonous snakes.

Only two among the dozens of different groups of centipedes have luminous species. This situation is analogous to that found among the beetles, whose huge order of Coleoptera contains only a few families with

A European species of luminous centipede.

luminous members. The big difference is that many luminous centipedes are blind, or have only the most rudimentary organs of sight, and cannot see the light they themselves produce. Because of this, we know that the light cannot possibly serve as a means of identification within the species—for example, attracting the opposite sex. Hence, biologists assume that the light is used by the centipedes to repel their enemies. The fact that these blind creatures secrete luminous substances supports the theory that the light serves as a defense mechanism. Up to this point, none of the luminescent animals we have met, with the exception of the still-not-completely-certified case of the tiger moth, possesses the ability to secrete luminous material. When combined with a repulsive odor and the capacity to burn or blister like acid on touch, such glowing secretions can act as an efficient deterrent. Centipedes have been observed scattering the shining slime all over animals which annoyed or threatened them. It seems logical to assume that any predator, after one or two such painful or at least unpleasant experiences, will in the future refrain from trying to make a meal of these crawling lights.

Luminous centipedes have been found in many parts of the world, among them Europe, Africa, and the East Indies. After the great volcanic explosion of 1883 on the island of Krakatoa off Java, luminescent centipedes, which had not been seen before, were observed. The upheaval had probably driven them from their usual hiding places.

The luminescence of millipedes, which belong to the Diplopoda, is also believed to be an instrument of self-defense, acting as a deterrent against attacks by predators. Despite their name, these many-legged creatures do not necessarily have ten times as many legs as centipedes, and no species has a thousand of them.

The first reliable report of a luminous millipede came in 1939 from Truk Island in the Pacific. This creature is said to emit a weak bluish luminescence which becomes stronger if the millipede is irritated. Because the species seems to be quite rare, observation and study have been limited, and more research is needed on this little-known type of luminescence.

Much more spectacular because of its larger size and stronger light is a millipede discovered as recently as 1949 in the North American West and apparently occurring only in a relatively small area. The first specimens were picked up by botanists exploring the region adjacent to California's famed Sequoia National Park. Puzzled by the unusual creatures, they turned them over to the biology department at the University of California. The millipedes were about an inch and a half long, and described as having a pale salmon pink or tan color.

Dr. Demarest Davenport, the biologist who received the millipedes, became quite excited after he had had a chance to study them closely. He had never seen and did not know of the existence of this species. What was more, even after the most diligent research, he could not find a record of any other naturalist having de-

A common European millipede.

scribed these millipedes, although they were quite distinctive. Especially in the dark, they glowed with what Dr. Davenport reported to be a "brilliant greenish-white fire." This luminescence came from practically all parts of the animal, including the antennae, the legs, and the edges of the dorsal plates. The light never went out during the life of the animal and shone steadily at all times, proving it was not under the nervous control of the millipede, and differing significantly from the light of such insects as the fireflies and the New Zealand glowworm.

As always in cases where luminescent species are reported, bacterial infection was at first suspected. However, as time went on and additional specimens were studied, this possibility became increasingly unlikely. Nevertheless, Dr. Davenport was not satisfied to rely only on his own research. He sent several specimens to other biologists and waited for their verdicts. The consensus finally confirmed his belief that these millipedes were a new kind never described before, that they constituted a new genus, having no immediate relatives, and that their luminescence was quite evidently "genuine"—meaning it was not caused by luminous bacteria.

Further investigation by Dr. Davenport into the life history of these odd creatures uncovered more interesting facts. *Luminodesmus sequoiae,* the name given to the newly discovered species, seems to be luminous even before the tiny larva hatches from the egg. Millipedes do not go through the four-stage metamorphosis —egg, larva, pupa, adult—found among advanced insects such as beetles, flies, and butterflies. They also do not have the simple development found in primitive insects whose young, called nymphs, are just like the adults but smaller and molt periodically as they grow. The development of millipedes is quite complicated and involves seven stages before they turn into mature adults. During the first larval stage they could be mistaken for insects because they have only six legs. *Luminodesmus* specimens were found to be luminous in every one of the six immature stages and as adults.

Although the light emitted by the California millipedes shines continually, its brightness is subject to fluctuation. As in the cases of other luminescent creatures, activity, stimulation, or a rise in the outside temperature increases the intensity of the glow. Conversely, a drop in temperature results in decrease in brightness.

Light-producing organs such as those found among fireflies and other luminescent insects are not present in *Luminodesmus.* Instead, the tissues that emit this light seem to be located in the lower layers of the hard, chitinous integument which forms a kind of external "skeleton" and protects the soft parts of the millipede's body.

Quite naturally, the question about a possible functional use for the luminescence of the California millipede arose immediately after the creatures had been established as self-luminous beyond a reasonable doubt. Biologists assume that the luminescence may serve a purpose similar to that of the centipedes: a warning device proclaiming the owner to be distasteful and better left undisturbed. The unpalatability of *Luminodesmus*, like that of other millipedes, results from a noxious gas containing cyanide which is produced by certain glands and emitted when danger appears to threaten. It might well be that the luminescence of this millipede takes over the warning role attributed to the bright colors of many distasteful insects. However, we must beware of trying to fit every phenomenon of living nature into our concept of functional usefulness.

So far, the Sequoia millipede is the only luminous member of its group found in North America. The fact that it was discovered at so late a date should encourage future biologists by making them aware that there is always a chance of discovering new and exciting animals even in our shrinking world.

As we descend the evolutionary ladder in search of other luminescent land creatures, we come next to the humble earthworms. Although these sightless burrowers serve a most useful purpose in nature's household because they constantly turn and aerate the soil, they are generally not considered especially interesting or colorful creatures. However, the earthworms, called Oligochaeta by biologists, include a number of luminous species, or, more accurately, species capable of secreting luminous material.

An earthworm is blind; in fact, it not only lacks eyes but does not even have a distinct head. As anyone who ever watched an earthworm knows, it is quite difficult to decide at times which is the front and which the hind end. Earthworms also cannot be distinguished by sex, because they are hermaphroditic, meaning that each individual has both male and female sex organs, a condition frequently found among invertebrates. Thus the light they produce obviously cannot serve as a means of attracting others of their kind.

The self-luminescence of certain earthworm species was once hotly debated among biologists, many of whom thought the light was caused by a bacterial infection. However, the latter theory has been disproved and genuine self-luminescence established beyond all

An earthworm secreting luminous material.

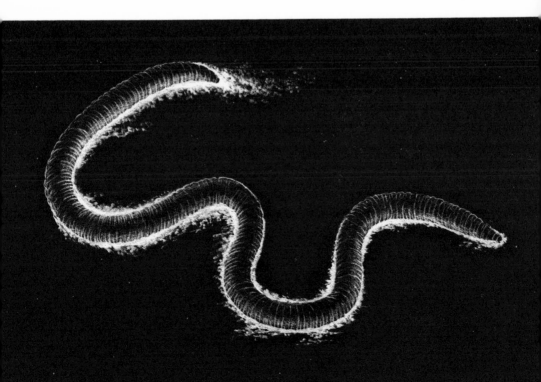

doubt. It seems that the earthworm's coelom, as the body cavity of these animals is called, secretes a substance which turns luminescent as it is exuded by the worm during its movements. Thus the earthworm leaves behind a trail of shining slime—to what purpose, no one has so far been able to say conclusively.

The largest and probably the most spectacular of all the luminescent earthworms is a species found in New Zealand, the home of so many other strange creatures. This worm, which has the imposing scientific name *Octochaetus multiporus,* grows to a length of eighteen inches with a body diameter of half an inch, thus having the proportions of a small snake rather than those of a worm. Its color varies from light pink to almost white, and it is generally found in heavy clay subsoil. The coelomic fluid secreted by this worm has a bright orange-yellow luminescence which retains its intensity for a considerable period of time after it has been exuded. Under ultraviolet light this substance fluoresces with a similar color, changing to blue shortly before the luminescence disappears altogether.

If the worm, which has translucent body-wall muscles, is handled or otherwise irritated, it exudes through the pores of its back as well as from all other body openings a sticky, brightly shining fluid, a fact which would indicate that the luminescence of this earthworm at least is an instrument of self-defense. How much of a deterrent against predators it is has not yet been established.

Among the most recently discovered crawling, land-

Dyakia striata, *a rare luminous snail.*

living light producers is a snail that was, like the Sequoia millipede, observed only about twenty years ago. It was found by Dr. Yada Haneda, a well-known Japanese biologist who specializes in bioluminescence and has worked closely with American biologists in this field. The snail, whose scientific name is *Dyakia striata,* is native to the Malay Peninsula, and it is very similar to other snails except for the fact that it gives off a bluish light from an area just below its head. If irritated or attacked, the mollusk begins to flash this light off and on, thereby possibly scaring off some predators, who may find its display of pyrotechnics too strange to consider it an inviting morsel of food. The suspicion that the light could be due to bacterial infection has apparently proved groundless; it is generally accepted by scientists that *Dyakia striata* is self-luminous.

Although other luminescent land creatures may be discovered, the great majority of these animals undoubtedly are known today to biologists. At most, they are a relatively small group of only a few dozen genera. This is not true, however, of the light-producing animals that live in the ocean. In the next chapter we shall get some idea of the incredible variety of luminescent marine creatures already known to us, and the reasons why it is likely that many more are still unknown, waiting to be discovered and studied by enterprising naturalists of the future.

Lamps of the Sea

In the oceans of the world have been found a teeming variety of animal life, including the most primitive one-celled animals, so miniscule they become visible only under the microscope, animals that look like plants, highly specialized creatures, and the biggest and some of the most intelligent mammals in the world. Even so, we have not yet been able to study marine animal life as we have studied the majority of land animals. Deep-sea exploration is a relatively young branch of natural science. In the past few decades, the diving adventures of such explorers as Jacques-Yves

Cousteau and Georges Houot have brought us new, exciting discoveries about the strange life of the deep, where fairy-tale creatures and incredibly shaped monsters live in eternal darkness. There is so much more to be discovered, explored, and studied in the ocean depths that entire generations of naturalists will find rewarding fields of adventure—always provided that we can protect our oceans, along with the rest of our natural environment, from the steadily increasing dangers of pollution.

Whereas luminous land forms are the exception and are limited to a very few animal groups, luminous species in the ocean are found in practically all the larger groups. On the land, light-producing creatures are small and confined mostly to insects and their relatives. In the ocean, luminous forms are so prevalent, especially at the greater depths, that the noted American naturalist William Beebe estimated that more than ninety per cent of all deep-sea creatures have some type of luminescence. Light-producing marine animals do not, however, occur exclusively in the depths of the ocean; a great many luminous organisms are found in shallow waters or near the surface.

Most fish with true luminescence are inhabitants of the deep sea. They are not often seen near the shores or at the surface, and when they are, it is only because of special circumstances such as in a storm or during mating in shallower waters. The notion that the number of luminescent forms increases with the distance from the ocean surface is true only up to a certain point. There is a limit to the depth at which luminosity occurs; at depths of three miles, for example, the fish that live in these ocean abysses have lost practically all organs of sight, and with them the main reason for luminosity.

The largest animals proven to be luminescent are members of the group that includes sharks and dogfish. The first detailed report of a luminous shark dates from 1840. A few years earlier, the animal had been captured in the waters off Brazil and had been kept alive for a short time in an aquarium. An Englishman who wrote a book on a whaling expedition saw the shark and described it as glowing in the dark with a greenish light on its entire underside, including that of the head.

Biologists agree that this was a self-luminescent species. Many other deep-sea sharks and dogfish have since been found to produce light. The light organs of these fish are located in the skin and are comparable to those of other, unrelated marine creatures. Light emanating from the photophores, or light cells, is directed outward by reflector cells located directly beneath the light-producing tissues. In many other fish, the light organs are quite different.

Spinax niger is a luminescent dogfish found frequently in the waters off Japan. Its species name, which means "black," is descriptive of the very dark color of its back and the numerous black stripes and irregular areas on its belly and sides when seen in daylight. These areas are covered by pigment cells, or chromatophores, beneath which lie the photophores. In the dark-

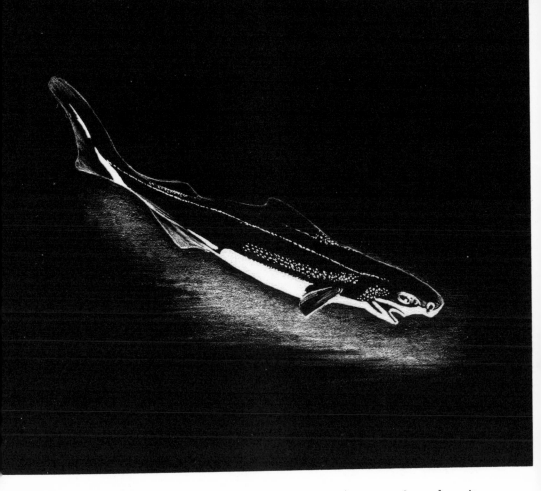

A brilliantly luminescent shark. All light organs are located on its underside.

ness, however, these pigment cells contract, exposing the luminescent organs, whose greenish light then shines forth, directed downward, as in many other luminescent marine animals. Exactly why this is so nobody knows for sure, although different theories have been advanced. One theory interprets the light that shines downward as a defense against predators that lurk below, watching for the dark shadows of their prey swimming above them. Other scientists think it helps the luminescent animals to find food more easily. Most biologists agree, however, that the variations in size, number, and shape of the light organs serve as a means of identification and recognition. Most luminescent fish have functional eyes and are therefore well able to see the light produced by others like themselves.

Grotesque shapes which, in combination with the light they emit, give them a bizarre, "other-world" appearance are common among luminous fish. *Argyropelecus*, for example, popularly called the hatchetfish, is a strange little creature found in ocean depths around the world. Numbers of these fish can sometimes be seen on shores after having been cast up by depth-scouring tides. Described by one naturalist as a "miniature monster with a harlequin mask," the hatchetfish is silvery and partly transparent, with huge eyes and a thin, flat body. Although it is only about two inches long, the big mouth that can be opened wide enough to swallow prey not much smaller than the fish itself is an indication of its fiercely predaceous nature. Its most outstanding feature, however, is the luminescence coming from rows of jewel-like organs located on the underside of its thin belly. These organs appear pink when seen in reflected light. In the dark they give off a bright glow. While diving in the Strait of Messina with his bathyscaphe, the modern vehicle for deep-sea exploration, French marine scientist Lieutenant Commander Georges Houot observed the fish he later described as "sparkling like torches" as they swam along in the

A species of Argyropelecus, *or hatchetfish, found in ocean depths in many parts of the world.*

darkness of the underwater world.

Another strange-looking luminescent inhabitant of the deep sea is *Stomias columbrinus,* a slender but large-headed fish with two rows of lighted "portholes" along its sides, a light under each eye, and a luminous barbel—a tactile appendage—under its jaw. The barbel is also supposed to serve as bait for the small creatures on which *Stomias* feeds. From the lower "battery," this fish can direct a solid sheet of light downward.

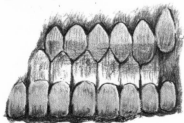

Close-up of the light organs of the hatchetfish.

Myctophum coccoi was discovered by William Beebe, who found it fascinating. The fish has about fifty individual lights, with thirty-two on the belly and twelve on the sides. All these lights can be flashed independently.

Other luminescent species include sunfish and toadfish. Popularly called midshipmen, toadfish are frequently seen in aquaria. So far, however, there has been an almost universal failure to get any fish to luminesce in captivity. Why this should be so, we still do not know. Attempts to stimulate the normally luminous species into emitting light have been successful in some cases either by adding certain chemicals to the water or by subjecting the fish to electric shocks. Further research and study will probably solve the difficulty and permit aquaria in the future to create conditions so closely resembling the natural habitats of these fish that they will emit light as freely in captivity as they now do in the open sea.

Rows of lights along the sides are the main characteristic of the deep-sea Stomias columbrinus.

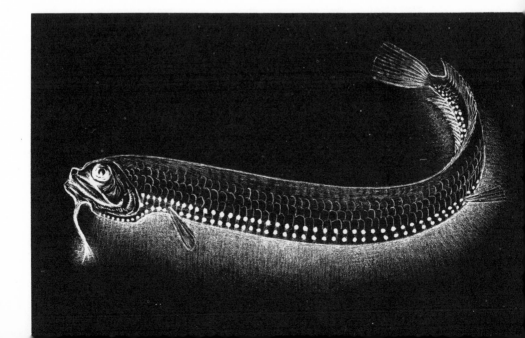

An interesting fact about the luminosity of fish as compared to that of other marine creatures is the color of the light, which seems to be greenish-white or yellow in the majority of cases. As we shall see, this limitation of colors does not hold true for other luminescent marine organisms.

We cannot end the discussion on luminous fish without mentioning those that lack light-producing organs but still are capable of emitting light because they harbor in their bodies colonies of luminous bacteria. This condition has nothing in common with the fatal infection by luminous bacteria described in the preceding chapters, as the colonies of bacteria that inhabit fish live in a symbiotic relationship with their hosts. In other words, the fish and the bacteria live together in a relationship that is mutually beneficial, or at least not harmful to the host fish. While it is not quite clear yet how the fish benefits from the presence of the bacteria, several theories have been advanced. The advantage for the bacteria, of course, is easily understood.

There is a fish known as *Malacocephalus*—literally, "soft-headed"—which has a gland in its abdomen that harbors luminous bacteria. The body juices of the fish supply nourishment for the bacteria. By a special mechanism, *Malacocephalus* is able to squeeze out into the surrounding water large numbers of these bacteria, thus illuminating its surroundings. It is thought that the shining water possibly attracts some of the smaller marine creatures on which the fish feeds.

Another instance of symbiosis between a fish and

Luminous deep-sea fish. ▶

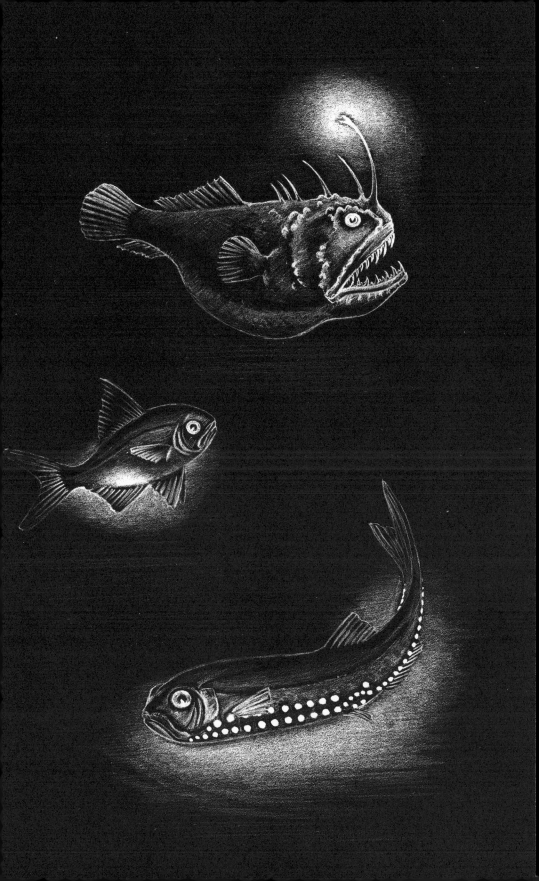

luminous bacteria is *Photoblepharon*, found in the waters around Indonesia. This otherwise normal-looking fish has large pouches under its eyes. These bags are filled with colonies of luminous bacteria, which remain there throughout the life of the fish and are fed by an intricate system of capillaries supplying nutrition to the light-producing "guests." It is thought that *Photoblepharon* uses the light to blind rather than to attract its prey.

Because luminous bacteria shine constantly, the fish that house these organisms have to swim around carrying illumination even at times when it is to their advantage to be dark and thus unseen. In *Photoblepharon* there is a very handy device by which the fish, though unable to turn off the bacteria's light, is able to prevent the light from shining outward. This mechanism consists of a "shutter," a lightproof membrane which can be moved at will by the fish, sliding across the pouches in much the same way as we pull down a blind at night to prevent light from shining out a window.

Both the squid and the fish in this illustration have symbiotic relationships with luminous bacteria living in their bodies. The squid ejects the bacteria, whereas the fish harbors them in special pouches.

Symbiosis with luminous bacteria is by no means limited to fish. Quite a few species of squids, for example, house such bacteria in their bodies. Some of these animals, which are members of the Cephalopoda, the highest class of mollusks, have special organs which provide shelter and nourishment for luminous bacteria. *Sepiola,* for instance, has a saclike organ located beneath the head at the point where it joins the body, in which its luminous bacteria live and thrive. Whenever it feels the need, the *Sepiola* sprays out some of the bacteria in a shining, pale-blue mass which illuminates the surrounding water. It is assumed that this luminescent cloud is a defensive measure and serves to distract and confuse potential enemies. It thus would fulfill a purpose similar to the dark, inky fluids discharged by many squids and squid relatives, which provide "smoke screens" facilitating their escape when threatened.

Squids living in a symbiotic relationship with luminous bacteria have the same problem as fish who enjoy a similar arrangement: the light of the bacteria shines constantly, even at times when the host animal may prefer to be dark. Although squids do not have a specialized device like the shutter with which *Photoblepharon* controls the bacterial light, they do possess the means of preventing the light from shining outward: the gland containing the bacteria can be enveloped in a dense, dark fluid.

Not all squids that emit light rely on bacteria for their illumination; on the contrary, they are outnumbered by truly self-luminous species. Among the latter we find variations in the way luminescence is achieved. While most have light organs, a few discharge a luminescent secretion whose chemical make-up is designed to produce light the moment it comes into contact with the oxygen present in water. As the mucus is ejected by the animal, it turns into shining threads or whorls displaying a bluish or greenish luminescence.

Thaumatolampas diadema, *the jeweled squid, seen from above in daylight (left) and in darkness with its lights in operation.*

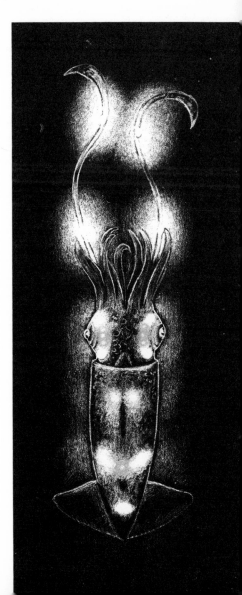

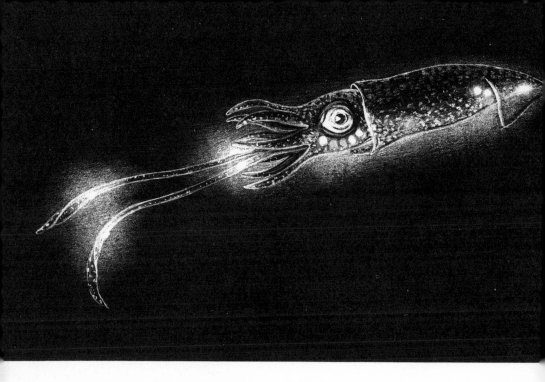

The jeweled squid in its deep-sea habitat.

The most spectacular as well as the most colorful of all the luminescent squids are those with actual light organs. They are all deep-sea dwellers, which is not necessarily true of those discussed earlier, some of which may be found relatively close to the surface.

The variations in the number, size, arrangement, and color of the photophores among the deep-sea species of squids are remarkable. One of the most beautiful, *Thaumatolampas diadema,* the jeweled squid, is found in the depths of the Indian Ocean and displays lights of three different colors. The huge eyeballs of *diadema* are accented by five photophores which shine in pearly gray and blue. On the underside of the body the squid bears eight more lights, which glow with a ruby-red in the front, blue in the middle, and white at the rear end. Naturalists agree that this squid with all its lights on provides a magnificent spectacle.

Some tiny squids display an incredible number of light organs. One four-inch species from New Zealand has no fewer than ninety photophores, seventy of them on its long tentacles and arms. Others have only a few, but almost always there are some on or around the eyes.

A very pretty luminescent squid is a Japanese species called *Watasenia scintillans*. Its popular name is firefly squid. Only five inches long, this little creature has

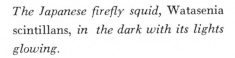

The Japanese firefly squid, Watasenia scintillans, *in the dark with its lights glowing.*

photophores on its eyes, on the tips of its ventral arms, and scattered irregularly over its entire body. In daylight these photophores look black, being covered by chromatophores that react to outside sources of light in the same way as described earlier in the case of *Spinax niger*. In the dark, the light of the firefly squid is very brilliant and has a bluish tint.

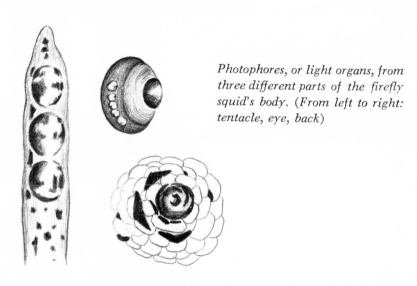

Photophores, or light organs, from three different parts of the firefly squid's body. (From left to right: tentacle, eye, back)

Huge numbers of these squids are caught every year by Japanese fishermen in late spring in the waters around Toyoma Bay. That is the time when these dwellers of the deep rise to the surface for their mating rituals. A netful of these star-studded little creatures is said to be an unforgettable sight.

It is somewhat surprising, in view of the many species of luminous squids, that their relatives, the octopuses, have practically no light-producing members. Only a

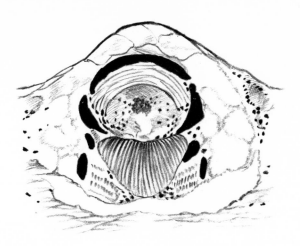

Light organ of a luminous squid.

single species has so far been reported to have a few luminescent organs on its arms.

We have seen that certain annelid, or segmented, worms living on the dry land are capable of secreting luminous substances. Their marine relatives include members that can put on a spectacular display of luminescence. Naturalists are fairly sure that worms belonging to the genus *Odontosyllis* were the shining lights, the "moving candles of the sea," which made so great an impression upon Christopher Columbus shortly before he landed in the New World.

Odontosyllis enopla, often called the Bermuda fireworm, is a free-swimming species which displays its light only in the breeding season. At this time the female quite suddenly becomes luminescent on the posterior three quarters of her body. Swimming near the surface, she begins to move in circles, throwing off eggs together with a brilliantly luminous substance that lights up the surrounding water. At that point, the

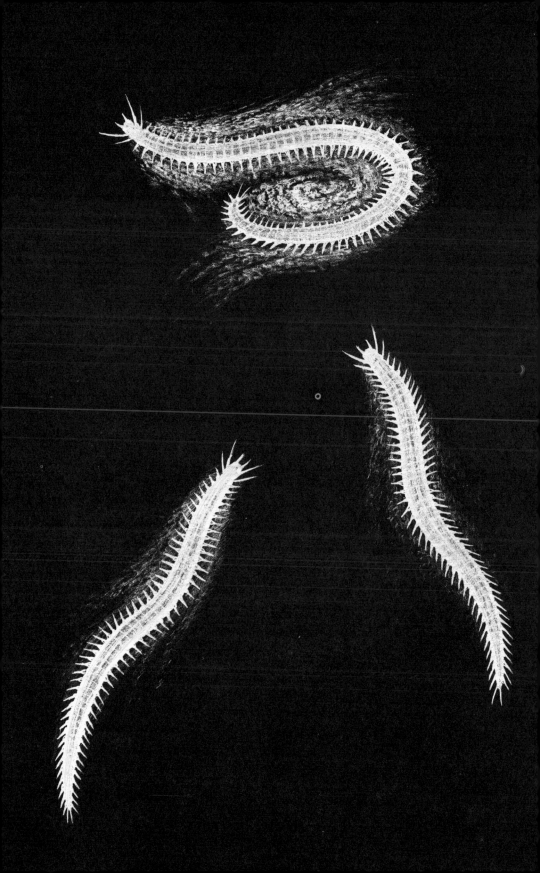

males come up from the depths. Locating the female by her light—and lighting up himself as he swims to the surface—a male will approach her, and the two then begin a strange kind of "dance" in which they rotate in the midst of the luminous area. During these movements the male scatters his sperm in the water and over the eggs. This mission completed, the worms turn dark again and soon after disappear into deeper waters.

The light emitted by *enopla* is a rich golden color, while that of other species is reported to have a greenish-blue hue. Prerequisite for the mating ritual of all these worms seems to be the absence of daylight; they do not begin to luminesce until after dark.

Another annelid worm native to many parts of the world has a pronounced, though normally hidden, luminescence. A strange creature called the paddleworm, it is found buried in the mud and sand near the shores of quiet ocean inlets. It spends its entire life in a U-shaped tube fashioned of its own secretions, which it never leaves and in which it can move about freely. In fact, the tube makes so roomy a home for the worm that quite often a number of crustaceans and other worms live in a peaceful symbiotic relationship with the paddleworm. The scientific name of the genus is *Chaetopterus*.

Taken from its tube, the worm reveals so fantastic a shape that it looks more like some sort of nightmare creature than a real animal. Only about four inches long, it appears to have been put together from parts belonging to several different animals.

◄ *Mating ritual of the Bermuda fireworm,* Odontosyllis enopla.

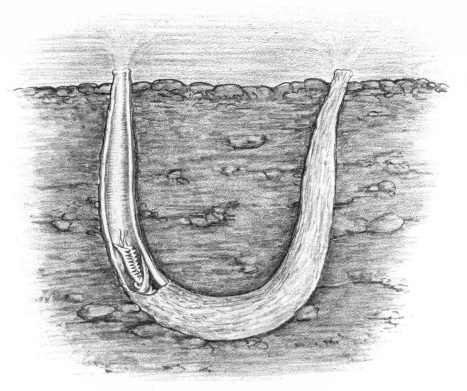

The paddleworm in its partially opened parchment tube.

This worm shines with a greenish-blue light resulting from fine clouds of luminous material which it secretes. The glowing substance is produced by the skin tissues of the worm and comes off on the fingers of anyone who

The paddleworm removed from its tube.

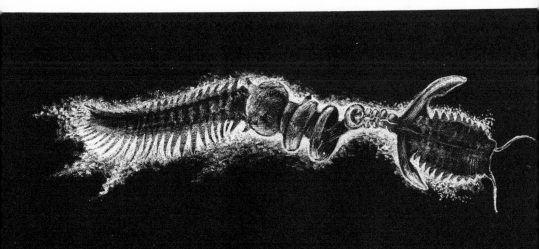

handles it. Although the hidden light of *Chaetopterus* is believed to have some sort of defensive value, eels often pull these worms from their tubes and eat them without the slightest hesitation. It is therefore difficult to say whether the luminescence has any functional use as we understand it.

The large class of the crustaceans has quite a number of luminescent species, mainly among the very small, primitive members of the group. The largest and most advanced of light-producing crustaceans seem to be the various luminous deep-sea shrimp species. One three-inch red shrimp has a number of light organs along the sides, covered by chromatophores in daylight, but it also possesses the ability to emit clouds of luminous material when frightened.

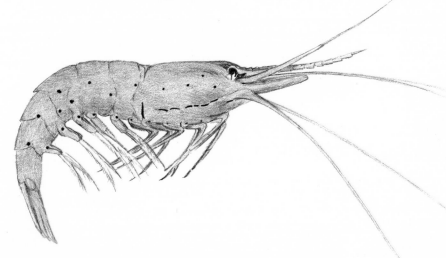

The light organs of this shrimp, seen here in daylight, appear as small black dots and dashes.

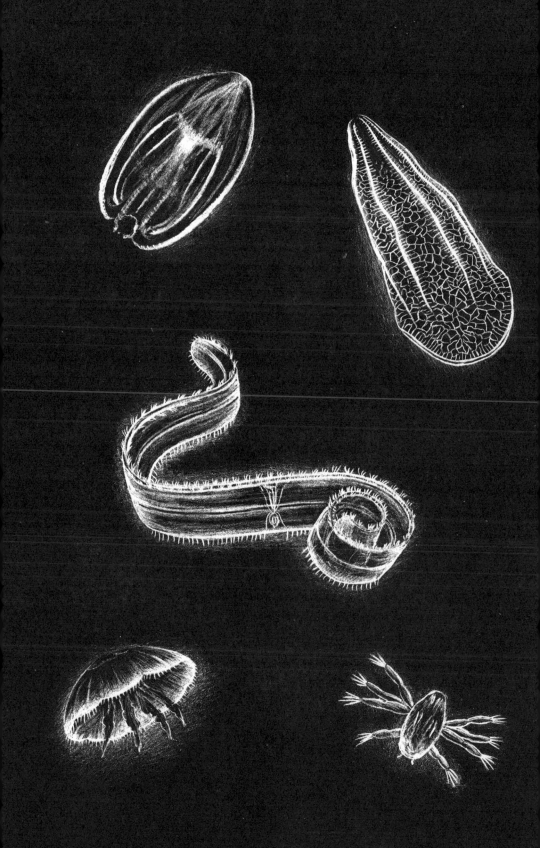

Among the ostracods and the copepods, both of which are groups of primitive crustaceans, luminescent species are numerous. These creatures are very small, but in great numbers their luminescence provides quite a display. They, together with such organisms as jellyfish, comb jellies, and tunicates, are the animal constituents of plankton, the minute ocean life on which so many other ocean creatures feed, and much of which displays the luminescence at or near the surface of the ocean that has been viewed with wonder—and, in past times, with superstitious awe—by sailors and others who watched the waters glow with an eerie light at night.

Not all luminescent jellyfish are tiny. Some attain a size of a few inches across and shine with a bluish or violet light from a great number of spots along the lower edges of their domes. They occur in oceans around the world and have been found in the coldest waters and even beneath the ice. The light they emit is not dependent upon warm temperatures and will shine as brightly in the Arctic Current as in warm tropical waters.

Finally we come to the smallest of the light-giving ocean creatures, the microscopic, mostly one-celled organisms called protozoa, many of which move about with the help of tiny tails or "whips." Some of these organisms, at the borderline between plant and animal life, are very interesting because, though tiny, they have the ability to produce light. They have become famous for the color they give the ocean by day and the glow they add by night whenever a wave or some

Various small luminescent marine creatures.

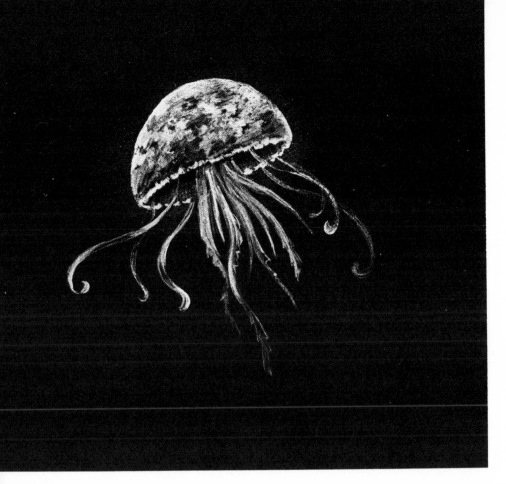

A large luminous jellyfish.

other movement disturbs the waters. Because of their huge numbers, which are not in the millions but in the billions and trillions, they are able to create the shining surf that can be seen along many shores on autumn nights.

Among the best known of the microscopic luminescent organisms are *Noctiluca miliaris* and several species of the genus *Gonyaulax*. These organisms have been subjected to extensive tests by scientists, and many interesting facts about the process that produces their luminescence have been established, as we shall see in a later chapter. One of the most intriguing problems is posed by the fact that the *Gonyaulax* species have a built-in rhythm which permits them to dim their lights during the twelve-hour period of daylight and then to shine again in the twelve nighttime hours. When, as a test, the organisms were kept twenty-four hours a day in artificial light, they still dimmed their lights in alternate twelve-hour periods regardless of the fact that there was no variation of light in the laboratory in which they were kept!

In addition to the many swimming and floating lights of the ocean, there are a considerable number of luminescent marine creatures that never move around but remain anchored to the bottom of the ocean, looking more like plants than animals. In the chapter that follows, we will take a look at the strange glowing life of the ocean floor.

Shining Underwater Gardens

The free-swimming inhabitants of the ocean are not the only ones that are able to give off light. The sand and rocks of the ocean floors near reefs and shores are populated by a great variety of creatures which are either anchored to the bottom and are unable to move at all, or whose movements are severely restricted. Many of these groups have luminous members; in fact, some of the most beautifully fluorescent of all living organisms are found on the ocean floor along coral reefs, and their ability to give off light was unknown until a little more than a decade ago.

The luminescence of many bottom dwellers, on the other hand, has been known and observed since ancient times. A few of them are luminous only when they are externally stimulated—when something or someone touches them, for example. In others the glow is more or less continuous, even though stimulation almost always increases the intensity of the light. Among the more or less stationary mollusks, the luminescent clams are perhaps the best known. The genus *Pholas* has a special claim to fame, for clams of this type were well known to the ancient Romans, who considered them a great delicacy. The historian Pliny the Elder, who was very much interested in natural history and to whom we owe many descriptions of animal life as it was observed in those times, wrote that these clams often shone in the mouths of the dinner guests whom wealthy Romans liked to entertain with rare and expensive foods.

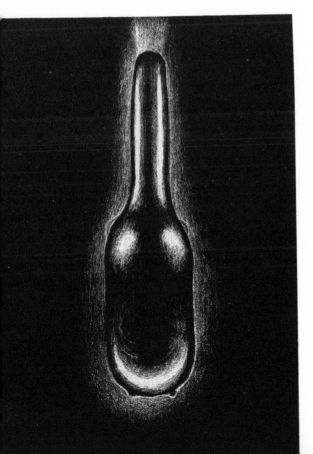

Pholas *clam without its shell, showing areas of luminescence.*

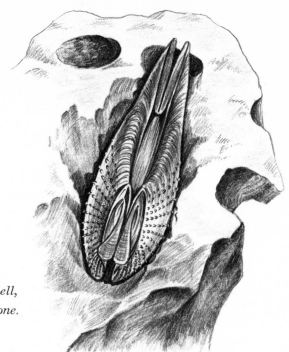

Pholas *clam in its shell,*
boring its way into stone.

Different species of *Pholas* occur in various parts of the world. They are sold commercially as "piddocks." This bivalve mollusk can dig deep into hard-packed mud, or even rock, by using the rasplike edges of its shell as a drill, wriggling around until it makes a hole large enough to accommodate it. Then it thrusts out its finger-like "neck" to siphon in the sea water that contains the minute organisms on which it lives.

The luminescence of this clam is quite pronounced. The glowing areas differ somewhat, but all the luminous species emit a bluish-tinted light and have the ability to emit luminous secretions into the surrounding water, especially when they are strongly stimulated externally.

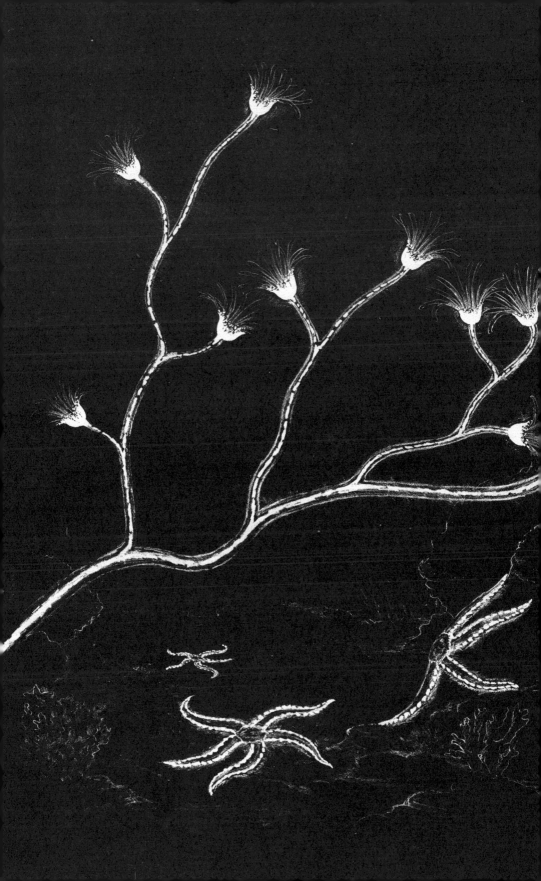

It is interesting to note that the only fresh-water animal proved to be self-luminescent is also a member of the mollusk group. It is a limpet, found in rapid streams in New Zealand. This mollusk is able to secrete luminous material into the water. The light has a bluish hue similar to that of the luminous clams.

Of the creatures that usually move around on the ocean floor searching for food, luminescent sea slugs and starfish are among the brightest. The marine snail *Phyllirrhoe bucephala* flickers all over with a strong greenish light at the least stimulation, and luminous five-armed starfish make beautiful shining patterns on the sand of the ocean floor.

The most spectacular of all nonswimming luminous marine creatures are certain kinds of plantlike animals that are firmly anchored to one spot; they come in a variety of wonderful shapes that, outlined by their luminescence, makes the bottom of the sea seem like a fairy-tale garden in the dark. They are mostly colonies of small animals living together, usually inside beautifully shaped "skeletons," which provide them with homes and which they build from lime and certain other substances. These organisms include the sea pens, or sea feathers, the hydroids, sea anemones, sponges, and corals. Each of these groups includes at least some species capable of producing light.

Luminosity of the sea pens has been known for a very long time. The German naturalist Konrad von Gesner, whose book on luminescence was mentioned in the first chapter, describes the sea pens in some de-

Luminous hydroids and starfish illuminate the ocean floor.

tail. A great many different species of sea pens, or pennatulids, as scientists call them, are luminous. The name "pennatulid" comes from the shape of these creatures, which look very much like feathers. Many of them grow to a considerable size. *Funiculina quadrangularis*, for example, attains a length of more than five feet, and each one of its blossom-like polyps, the tentacle-surrounded part that has the mouth opening at one end, is nearly an inch long. At the slightest touch, the lower part of the "stem," more than a foot in length, glows with what is described as a solid sheet of pale-green light, which flickers and races along the stem like a living thing. The polyps themselves in this species give off light only if they are more strongly stimulated.

Among the sponges, self-luminescence seems to be all but lacking. Only one species has yet been proved able to produce light. Many other sponges have in the past been reported as being luminous. Upon closer examination, however, they were found to harbor symbiotic colonies of other kinds of small marine creatures which, because of their luminosity, gave the sponge the appearance of shining with its own light.

The same, by the way, holds true for certain seaweeds that were once reportedly luminescent. They are beautiful to look at as they glow in the dark while gently swaying with the ocean currents. As in the case of the luminous sponges, the glow comes from small animals that have selected the plant as their permanent abode.

Luminous sea pens display their featherlike shape in the darkness.

Until recently the large group of corals, which were expected to yield many luminous forms, proved to be rather disappointing. Only horn corals, it seemed, had light-producing species. Horn corals look not at all like

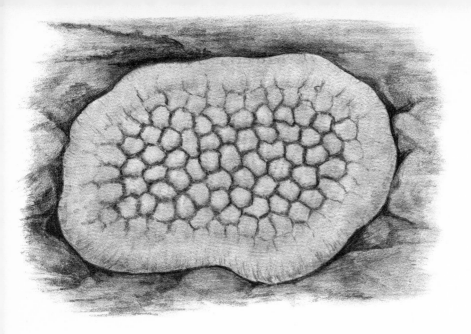

A large deep-sea coral in daylight.

the familiar types of coral. Some of them form rows of slender tubes reminiscent of organ pipes. A number of horn-coral species are luminous, giving off light that may have bluish or lilac hues.

Until about fifteen years ago, scientists assumed that the corals as a group had comparatively few luminescent members. Then divers exploring a Pacific reef came across deep-sea corals which emitted a soft light, each kind glowing with a different color. In the semi-darkness of the depths more than one hundred feet below the surface, these luminous corals turned the rocks and sand of the reef into magical shining gardens. But when the divers brought up some of the glowing corals, a sharp disappointment awaited them, for in daylight the corals were unattractive brown things, nor did they glow when placed in tanks and kept in the

dark. However, as soon as they were exposed to ultraviolet light, they began to fluoresce with the same
beautifully colored glow they had displayed on the
sand of the reef. Evidently, these corals react only to
ultraviolet light, and even though such light is present
in sunlight, the other rays have to be filtered out in
order for the ultraviolet to take effect. At the depths at
which these corals occur, practically all the rays of sunlight except the invisible ultraviolet radiation have
been filtered out by the water.

The story of how a great many fluorescent deep-sea
corals and sea anemones, some of them very rare, were
collected, photographed, and studied is a fascinating
account of an unusual nature adventure. It happened in
New Caledonia, an island off the coast of Australia in
the South Pacific.

Nouméa, the capital of New Caledonia, which used
to be a French penal colony, has a fine aquarium in
which much of the marine life of that part of the South
Pacific is on display. Dr. René Catala, the director of

Under ultraviolet light, this coral displays colored fluorescence.

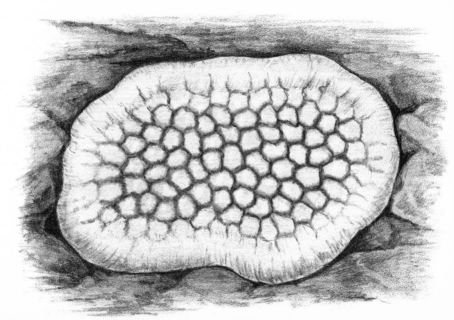

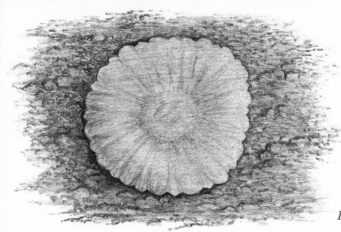
Deep-sea coral in daylight.

the aquarium, is a naturalist acutely aware of the unique beauty of the many creatures that inhabit the reefs and banks of that area and is devoted to the preservation and protection of this life against continuing encroachments by modern man.

Dr. Catala had been very much interested in the ability of marine creatures to emit fluorescent light under ultraviolet stimulation. His experiments with giant clams and other similar animals had been very disappointing and not at all what he had expected. Then, in 1957, Dr. Catala was commissioned by the government to examine a big reef near which an oil-exploration company had planned to dynamite in order to find out whether oil could be found under the ocean floor. Marine experts were worried about the effects of large-scale dynamiting on the marine life of the reef and wanted to make quite sure that any explosions would be limited to areas where relatively little damage would be caused.

After a sound-echo test, which showed a most interesting reef formation, Dr. Catala, assisted by experienced divers, began the job of exploring the reef and its animal population. The divers were sent down to depths of 100 to 120 feet and, in a series of diving trips, brought up a fascinating collection of marine creatures, especially corals. Some of the latter were extremely rare specimens.

Dr. Catala decided to test them all for possible fluorescent properties. This time he was not disappointed: many of the corals and some of the sea anemones, which in daylight had mostly dull colors, glowed with beautiful multicolored hues as soon as they were exposed to irradiation by the "black-light" (ultraviolet) lamps.

In the course of several additional diving expeditions, more corals, sea anemones, and starfish were brought up, in addition to other inhabitants of the reef. Again, most of the corals reacted with their wonderful colored fluorescence to stimulation by ultraviolet radiation.

Soon Dr. Catala had assembled a magnificent collection of color photographs of the fluorescent specimens illuminated by their own unearthly light. Arranged on the sand in suitable tanks and kept in the semi-darkness they were accustomed to, these strange creatures looked like an underwater garden of stemless flowers in every conceivable hue.

During his studies of these special organisms which had fluorescent properties, Dr. Catala made quite a few

The same coral after irradiation by ultraviolet light.

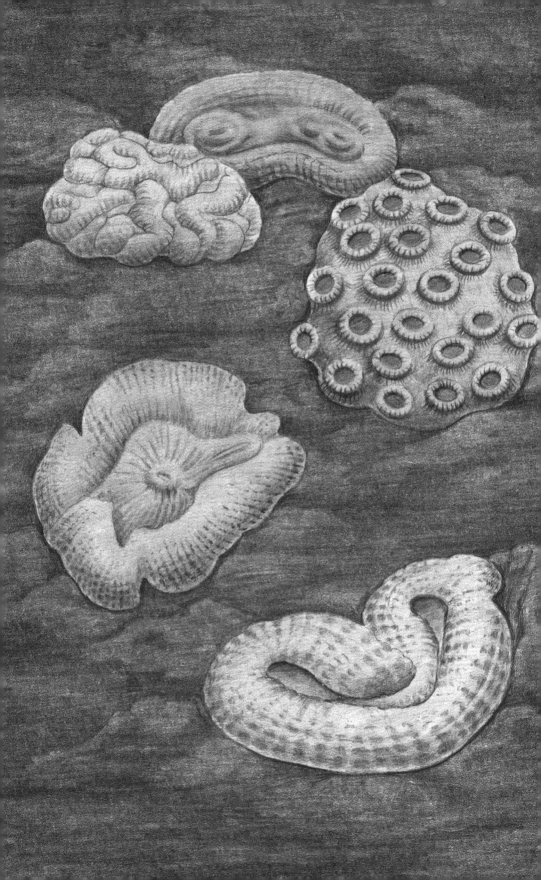

Luminescent deep-sea corals, stimulated by ultraviolet rays.

interesting observations. He found, for example, that only a very small number of corals respond to irradiation by fluorescing. He also found that individuals of a particular group emit light of the same, or at least very similar, color. Also, the colors could be grouped according to the frequency of occurrence. Thus he found that greens of all different hues predominated. After green came orange, and then the different shades of yellow— pale, dark, and golden. This was followed by blue and bluish, including lilac and violet hues. Red and reddish tones were relatively rare, both bright and dull shades. The rarest of all were the achromatic, colorless hues such as brown, beige, and gray.

The fact that only the live parts of the corals displayed the colored light was proof that the fluorescence was a true bioluminescence, not a chemical reaction of the inorganic material of the "skeletons" to ultraviolet light.

Further experimentation showed that irradiation with ultraviolet light affects these organisms in a number of other ways. For example, it keeps the polyps of corals expanded even in complete darkness, despite the fact that these polyps are normally open only by day. It also increases the turgidity, or swelling, of the sea anemones' tentacles. Too much radiation, however, is bad for the corals, tends to make them sickly, and changes the color of the emitted light. Large doses of irradiation over prolonged periods proved fatal to corals of certain groups. On the other hand, small doses of ultraviolet light are tolerated well and for considerable lengths of time. Under the stimulation of such irradiation, the underwater gardens shine forth with all their magnificent many-hued light.

Quite naturally, the fluorescent properties of Dr. Catala's deep-sea corals aroused great interest in scientific circles, and these organisms have since been subjected to considerable investigation and study. As a result it has been found that the location of the fluorescent cells differs in the various genera. Those of green corals, for example, are located in the ectodermic, or outer, skin layers in a few genera, and in the endodermic, or lower, layers in others. Some corals may have fluorescent cells distributed throughout the entire ectoderm, but in many they are confined to certain areas.

Although studies on the fluorescence of these corals are continuing, it has been established beyond doubt that the seat of the fluorescence is to be found in certain pigments which react to ultraviolet radiation by emitting light.

As word of Dr. Catala's collection spread, naturalists from many countries came to see and admire the display. So impressive was it that one zoologist suggested taking them to Europe so that people there would be able to get an idea of the beauty of these corals. At first Dr. Catala rejected the idea as unfeasible. Since the corals had to get constantly renewed sea water in order to survive, a long air trip seemed out of the question. However, after a series of experiments he devised a way which he believed offered a good chance of getting the

delicate creatures safely halfway around the world to Belgium, where his friend was director of the zoo at Antwerp.

After a trip with stopovers in many countries and with continuous checks on the conditions of the corals in plastic bags filled with sea water, the plane carrying Dr. Catala and his precious cargo finally landed in Antwerp, where a group of scientists and public officials stood ready to greet him. Placed on air mattresses during the car ride to the aquarium, the corals survived the trip, and they were soon arranged in suitable tanks and put in semidarkness to simulate their natural environment. Finally the ultraviolet lamps were turned on, and there, before the eyes of the delighted Belgians, the underwater lights shone forth with all the splendor of their jewel colors.

In the following weeks, visitors from all parts of Belgium and from many other countries saw the display. King Leopold of Belgium, who was one of the first to visit the aquarium, asked Dr. Catala how long the corals would survive. His estimate of only three or four weeks turned out to be a little pessimistic, as the corals lived for more than two months. During this time thousands of visitors had a chance to see their exquisite beauty, thereby securing a broader popular interest in the efforts of marine biologists and conservationists to preserve the unique underwater life of the world's reefs, shores, and ocean floors.

No one yet has been able to find any functional explanation for the fluorescence of the deep-sea corals.

Whatever their possible function, all we know today is that they are beautiful. For the time being we will have to accept the many-hued light of these creatures, along with many other "living lights," only as more evidence of the countless ways in which unknown forces of nature are able to express themselves.

The Anatomy of
Bioluminescence

When Robert Boyle, in 1667, put a piece of shining wood under a glass bell, removed the air with a pump, and watched the wood lose its glow and turn dark, he made the first big step toward solving the riddle of bioluminescence. There still remained a long, long way to go, and satisfactory answers to the question of how luminescent organisms manage to produce light would not be forthcoming until nearly three hundred years after Boyle's original experiment. The important fact established by that and similar experiments was that oxygen seems to be a vital ingredient for most, if not all, of the light produced by luminescent animals, as well as by plants.

The role of oxygen in the life processes of organisms on our planet is common knowledge: any creature that breathes needs a constant supply of oxygen to stay alive. As oxygen is inhaled, it combines in the tissues with other substances. This union of oxygen and other chemicals is called oxidation. It occurs in many forms: the relatively slow oxidation which takes place when we breathe; the very rapid oxidation, with its by-products of heat and light, of any fire; the extremely slow oxidation of metals such as iron to form rust. In all cases, some kind of combustion, or burning, takes place, and withdrawal of oxygen puts a stop to this combustion. The fact that withdrawal of air causes luminescence to cease in living tissues indicates that oxidation was involved in the production of "living light."

In the eighteenth and nineteenth centuries, scientists from many countries worked to find out more about bioluminescence. Their experiments confirmed the fact that oxygen was necessary for the emission of light by such diverse organisms as mushrooms, bacteria, fire-flies, and clams. These experiments also proved that, in many instances, the ability of the tissues to produce light lasted beyond the life of the animal. It was pos-sible to squeeze the juice from a luminescent clam, preserve it mixed with flour as a kind of patty, and make it shine again months later by placing it in warm water. Gradual heating of the water would increase the brightness of the light up to a certain point. At approximately 132 degrees Fahrenheit, all lumines-cence would cease, and nothing could thereafter bring it back.

Despite all the experiments and the wealth of fascinating facts that had been learned about various luminescent creatures, scientists a hundred years ago still did not know what went on in the light-producing tissues of luminous organisms, nor did they know what substances were involved, except that oxygen played an important role.

That was where matters stood toward the end of the nineteenth century when Dr. Raphael Dubois, a French physiologist, began in 1886 to examine luminescent organisms in his marine laboratory at Tamaris-sur-Mer in France.

Dubois had already worked with fire beetles, seeking to understand the process of their luminescence. Now he turned to a marine creature, the shining *Pholas* clam that had attracted attention even in ancient times.

Dubois extracted the juice of several *Pholas* clams, mixed it with cool water, and watched the solution shine for a while, then gradually fade and die. Then he mixed fresh clam juice with hot water but found that this mixture would not give off any light at all. Finally, in a flash of inspiration, he mixed the two non-luminous solutions, the one that had ceased to shine and the one that had never shown any sign of light. As soon as the two were combined, the bluish light typical of the *Pholas* clam shone forth once again. Obviously, the hot mixture and the cold one had each retained one necessary ingredient for luminescence while losing the other, so that they complemented each other when combined. In the cold-water mixture, one ingredient had been exhausted after a period of luminescence, while the hot water had destroyed a different ingredient in the second solution.

Dubois concluded that the substance destroyed by the hot water was most likely an enzyme, many of which are extremely sensitive to heat. An enzyme is a complex organic substance which in minute amounts promotes chemical change without itself being used up in the process. The word comes from the Greek word for "leaven." Enzymes are active in the fermentation of liquids and are known to chemists in that context as catalysts. In order to function, such catalysts need what is known as a substrate, a substance that reacts to a particular enzyme.

Dubois had now established that at least three ingredients were necessary to produce light such as that of fireflies or luminescent clams. One was an oxidizable substrate that needed a suitable catalyst, the second was that catalyst, the enzyme, and the third was oxygen, which, aided by the enzyme, combined with the substrate to create a form of combustion which released energy in the form of light.

It naturally fell to Dubois to name the substances which he had discovered. The names had to be very general terms, because both substrates and enzymes are chemically quite different in different animals. In other words, the enzyme of a fire beetle would not work with the substrate of a clam, and vice versa. The substances are similar only in the results they achieve as each pair combines with oxygen to produce light.

In order to coin descriptive terms, Dubois selected

the Latin word *lucifer*, which means "light-bringing" and which originally was applied to the morning star, the planet Venus. To this word he added the appropriate endings, naming the catalyst luciferase, because by that time the ending *-ase* was being used to designate enzymes. Zymase, for example, is a group of enzymes active in yeast. The substrate received the name luciferin.

The discovery of these biochemicals and their interaction was the beginning of decades of intensive research into the remaining mysteries of luminescence.

Much of this research in the first half of the twentieth century was done by Dr. E. Newton Harvey, professor of biology at Princeton University. In studies stretching over more than four decades and involving luminescent animals from many parts of the world, Dr. Harvey examined different kinds of luminosity. Among other things, he explained the process by which the secretions of certain animals light up as they are poured into the water in which these creatures live. It seems that the luciferin and the luciferase of these organisms are produced by different glands and are kept apart as long as they are in the body of the animal. Only when the substances meet after being ejected into the water, which contains the necessary free oxygen for the chemical union to take place, can light be produced.

In the past few decades, some of the most comprehensive research on luminescence has taken place at the McCollum-Pratt Institute for Trace Elements at Johns Hopkins University in Baltimore.

Dr. William D. McElroy, the director of the institute, became interested in luminescence when he worked at Princeton under Dr. Newton. After he was appointed director of the McCollum-Pratt Institute, he began a massive effort to penetrate the remaining secrets of bioluminescence.

In order to get enough firefly luciferin, which he especially wanted to study, he initiated an unprecedented firefly-collecting campaign, enlisting the help of hundreds of youngsters. In those years fireflies were caught and killed for experimental use in incredible numbers—sometimes nearly a million in a single summer season. Such slaughter, combined with the adverse effect of insecticides, has sharply reduced the number of these insects in many areas, a fact that is all the more regrettable because fireflies are useful predators as larvae and, as adults, lend their own irreplaceable magic to our summer nights. Nowadays, however, it is a lucky person who in the course of a summer sees even a few dozen fireflies twinkling in the bushes or against the night sky. As in countless other instances, man has interfered with a heavy and brutal hand and has destroyed what he should have helped preserve.

Dr. McElroy found that he needed more than two million fireflies in order to extract a single gram of luciferin. The powder gained by grinding dried firefly "tails" containing the light-producing organs was used for a variety of experiments.

As experimentation progressed, it became clear that other substances besides luciferin, luciferase, and oxygen were involved in the process resulting in light emission. Particularly one biochemical, commonly called ATP, played an important role. ATP's full name is "adenosine triphosphate," and it is as complex as it sounds. It is also a very interesting compound, for modern research has shown it to be present and active in most living creatures, whom it serves as a kind of "energy carrier."

Laboratory tests at Dr. McElroy's institute proved that ATP controls the brightness of the firefly's light: every additional dose of ATP made the light glow more brightly and with a more yellowish color. This biochemical thus has an effect similar to that of adrenalin, which, if injected into a live firefly, will make its light shine with a greatly increased brightness.

Because of its sensitive reaction to ATP, firefly extract is now being used to test the presence of very minute quantities of this biochemical in a variety of plant and animal tissues.

In 1961, scientists at the McCollum-Pratt Institute announced that they had succeeded in synthesizing luciferin. This meant that they had been able to put together the molecules of this organic substrate and thus duplicate it, and that it could be produced at any time in the laboratory in any desired quantity. At the same time, they claimed discovery of the answer to another one of the firefly's mysteries: its ability to turn its light off and then on again at will.

The question in this case was how the firefly manages to stay dark at times, even though the chemical ingredients for light production are all present and assembled in its light organs at all times. Logically, one would suppose it should glow constantly, like many other luminescent forms.

The answer to this riddle apparently is two substances also present in the firefly's abdominal tissues. One is a compound that prevents the luciferin-luciferase-oxygen interaction. So long as this chemical is active, the firefly's light remains turned off. When the insect's nerve impulses give the order to turn on the light, this signal releases another substance which acts upon the binder, preventing it from binding. At that moment, the oxidation process can take place, and the firefly's light shines forth. Then comes the order to turn off, and the supply of the substance inactivating the binding substance is stopped, the binding action is resumed, and the firefly is dark once more.

Through the research done by scientists such as those at the McCollum-Pratt Institute, we have come to understand much about many kinds of luminescence. Much, but by no means all. The chemistry that produces the firefly's glow is so complex, and so incredibly delicate, that it is not yet fully understood, and there also is no complete agreement among scientists about the way the flash is triggered and controlled. In addition, there are many forms of luminescence whose chemistry is quite unknown. In some of these cases, oxygen does not seem necessary for the production of light.

Future research will undoubtedly uncover many more

secrets of bioluminescence. Even those we already have solved let us marvel at the complexity of the process that produces the "living light." Today, bioluminescence is probed in many laboratories because of the possibility that it might lead us to the development of a form of light in which no energy would be wasted. In the meantime, however, the magic of these creatures that shine in the dark remains untouched for all those for whom the wonders of nature are much more than just an array of scientific facts.

Bibliography

Catala, René. *Carnival Under the Sea*. Paris: R. Sicard, 1964.

Harvey, E. Newton. *Bioluminescence*. New York: Academic Press, Inc., 1952.

———. *History of Luminescence from the Earliest Times until 1900*. Philadelphia: American Philosophical Society, 1957.

Johnson, Frank H., and Haneda, Yada, eds. *Bioluminescence in Progress*. Princeton: Princeton University Press, 1966.

Klein, H. Arthur. *Bioluminescence*. Philadelphia: J. B. Lippincott, Co., 1965.

Index

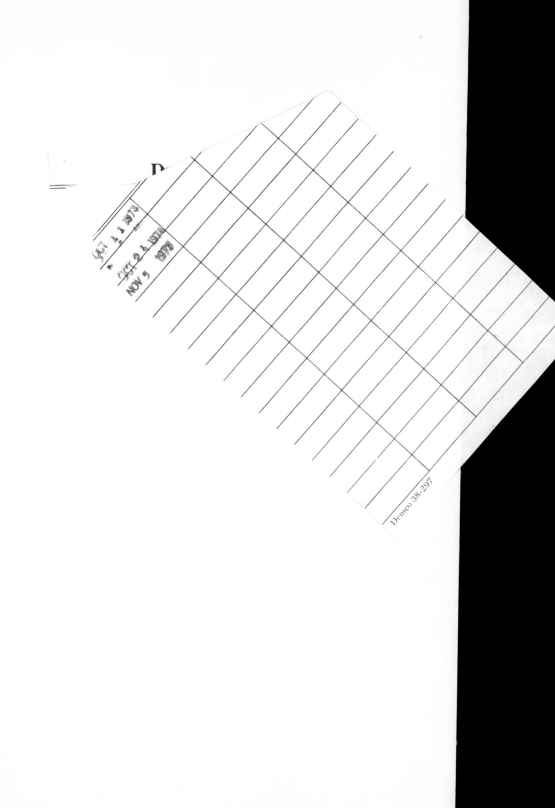